BEYOND RED STATE, BLUE STATE
ELECTORAL GAPS IN THE TWENTY-FIRST CENTURY AMERICAN ELECTORATE

REAL POLITICS IN AMERICA

Series Editor: Paul S. Herrnson, *University of Maryland*

The books in this series bridge the gap between academic scholarship and the popular demand for knowledge about politics. They illustrate empirically supported generalization from original research and the academic literature using examples taken from the legislative process, executive branch decision making, court rulings, lobbying efforts, election campaigns, political movements, and other areas of American politics. The goal of the series is to convey the best contemporary political science research has to offer in ways that will engage individuals who want to know about real politics in America.

BEYOND RED STATE, BLUE STATE
ELECTORAL GAPS IN THE TWENTY-FIRST CENTURY AMERICAN ELECTORATE

EDITED BY

Laura R. Olson
Professor of Political Science
Clemson University

John C. Green
Distinguished Professor of Political Science
Director, Ray C. Bliss Institute of Applied Politics
University of Akron

PEARSON
Prentice
Hall

UPPER SADDLE RIVER, NEW JERSEY 07458

Library of Congress Cataloging-in-Publication Data

Beyond red state, blue state : electoral gaps in the twenty-first century
American electorate / edited by Laura R. Olson, John C. Green.
    p. cm.
    Includes bibliographical references and index.
    ISBN-13: 978-0-13-615557-7
    ISBN-10: 0-13-615557-X
    1. Voting—United States. 2. Politics and culture—United States. 3.
Social choice—United States. 4. Political sociology. 5. Elections—United
States—History—21st century. I. Olson, Laura R. II. Green, John
Clifford.
    JK1967.B49 2008
    324.973—dc22

                  2007050228

Executive Editor:
  Dickson Musslewhite
Associate Editor: Rob DeGeorge
Editorial Assistant: Synamin Ballatt
Senior Marketing Manager:
  Kate Mitchell
Marketing Assistant: Jennifer Lang
Senior Managing Editor: Mary Carnis
Production Liaison: Debra Wechsler

Senior Operations Supervisor: Mary Ann Gloriande
Cover Art Director: Jayne Conte
Cover Design: Yellow Dog Designs
Cover Photo: Win McNamee/Getty Images
Composition/Full-Service
  Project Management: Laserwords/
  Katie Boilard, Pine Tree Composition, Inc.
Printer/Binder: R.R. Donnelley/Harrisonburg
Cover Printer: Phoenix

This book was set in 10/12 Palatino.

Real Politics in America
Series Editor: Paul S. Herrnson

Credits and acknowledgments borrowed from other sources and reproduced, with permission,
in this textbook appear on appropriate page within text.

Pearson Education LTD. London
Pearson Education Singapore, Pte. Ltd
Pearson Education, Canada, Ltd
Pearson Education–Japan
Pearson Education Australia PTY, Limited

Pearson Education North Asia Ltd
Pearson Educación de Mexico, S.A. de C.V.
Pearson Education Malaysia, Pte. Ltd
Pearson Education, Upper Saddle River,
  New Jersey

10 9 8 7 6 5 4 3 2 1
ISBN-(10):   0-13-615557-X
ISBN-(13): 978-0-13-615557-7

CONTENTS

PREFACE

Recent election-night media coverage has placed a heavy emphasis on coloring each state red or blue, depending on which party's candidate carries that state's electoral votes. We are left with the rather vivid impression that American voting behavior is somehow determined by citizens' state of residence. People who live in "red states" must vote Republican, while those who inhabit "blue states" must be Democrats. Understanding cleavages in American voting behavior is nowhere near this simple, however. A wide range of electoral gaps exists within the American electorate. These gaps distinguish citizens who vote Republican from those who vote Democratic on account of many basic demographic characteristics, such as race, gender, and social class.

This book represents an effort to explore the seven most politically significant demographic cleavages in American voting behavior today. We have assembled a team of contributors that includes leading scholars and political strategists, to analyze each of these electoral gaps in detail. Together they explore racial and ethnic gaps, the marriage gap, the worship attendance gap, the class gap, the rural–urban gap, the gender gap, and the generation gap. The book concludes with a look at how political campaigns make use of information about demographic gaps in the electorate.

We would like to thank the people who helped us see this project to completion. First and foremost, we thank the contributors to this volume for their excellent work, punctuality, and good cheer. The book began as an idea for a panel at the 2006 annual meeting of the Southern Political Science Association. We are grateful to Paul Herrnson for giving us the opportunity to convene the panel and for suggesting the idea for this book afterward. Thanks are also due to our editor at Prentice Hall, Dickson Musslewhite and his staff, especially Rob De George and Katie Boilard. We received support and input from our universities as well. Specifically, we thank the Department of Political Science at Clemson University and the Ray C. Bliss Institute of Applied Politics at the University of Akron. Joe Stewart, Paula McClain, Jeff Fine, Laura Stoker, Pei-te Lien, and Janet Bolois each offered their wisdom and assistance during various phases of this project. Finally, we thank our families and friends for their constant love and support.

About the Contributors

Paul A. Djupe is associate professor of political science at Denison University. His research has appeared in journals including the *American Journal of Political Science* and the *Journal of Politics*. He is coauthor of *The Prophetic Pulpit: Clergy, Churches, and Community in American Politics* (Rowman and Littlefield, 2003) and *Religious Institutions and Minor Parties in the United States* (Praeger, 1999); and coeditor of *Religious Interests in Community Conflict* (Baylor University Press, 2007) and *The Encyclopedia of American Religion and Politics* (Facts on File, 2003).

Amy Gershkoff received her Ph.D. in political science from Princeton University and is now Director of Analytics at MSHC Partners, where she develops micro-targeting strategies for political campaigns and nonprofit organizations. Prior to joining MSHC Partners, she worked as a polling consultant, providing strategic advice to campaigns and advocacy groups, and taught at Princeton University's Woodrow Wilson School and the City University of New York. Gershkoff's articles have been published in numerous media outlets and academic journals, including the *Christian Science Monitor*, *Perspectives on Politics*, *PS: Political Science and Politics*, and *The Democratic Strategist*. Gershkoff has been recognized as an "up and coming" leader in survey research by *Public Opinion Pros*, and was the recipient of the American Association of Public Opinion Research Seymour Sudman Award in 2005.

James G. Gimpel is professor of government at the University of Maryland. His research has appeared in the *Journal of Politics* and the *American Journal of Political Science*. Recent books include *Separate Destinations: Migration, Immigration, and the Politics of Places* (University of Michigan Press, 1999), as well as (as coauthor) *Cultivating Democracy: Civic Environments and Political Socialization in America* (Brookings Institution, 2003) and *Patchwork Nation: Sectionalism and Political Change in American Politics* (University of Michigan Press, 2003).

John C. Green is distinguished professor of political science and director of the Ray C. Bliss Institute of Applied Politics at the University of Akron, and Senior Fellow in Religion and Politics at the Pew Forum on Religion & Public Life, in Washington, DC. He is author of *The Faith Factor: How Religion Influences American Elections* (Praeger, 2007). He is also coauthor of *The Bully Pulpit: The Politics of Protestant Clergy* (University Press of Kansas, 1997), *Religion and the Culture Wars: Dispatches from the Front* (Rowman and Littlefield, 1996), and *The Diminishing Divide: Religion's Changing Role in American Politics* (Brookings Institution, 2000). In addition, he is coeditor of *The State of the Parties* (Rowman and Littlefield, 2003), now in its fifth edition, and *Multiparty Politics in America* (Rowman and Littlefield, 2002), in its second edition.

Anna Greenberg is Vice President of Greenberg Quinlan Rosner Research. She earned a Ph.D. in Political Science from the University of Chicago. She has been called "one of the smartest of the younger Democratic consultants" and is a leading polling expert. She advises campaigns, advocacy organizations, and foundations in the United States and has conducted groundbreaking research on both religion and values in public life and women's health. Greenberg directs Greenberg Quinlan Rosner's evolving work with Web-based research and its innovations in micro-targeting. Prior to joining Greenberg Quinlan Rosner, Greenberg taught at Harvard University's John F. Kennedy School of Government. She serves on the advisory board of the Boisi Center for Religion and American Public Life at Boston College and is a research fellow at American University's Center for Congressional and Presidential Studies.

Kimberly A. Karnes is a Ph.D. candidate in the Department of Government at the University of Maryland. Her interests include political behavior, elections, political geography, and rural and small-town politics.

Karen M. Kaufmann earned her Ph.D. in political science at UCLA and is currently an associate professor of government and politics at the University of Maryland, College Park. Her widely cited work on the gender gap has appeared in the *American Journal of Political Science, Public Opinion Quarterly, Political Behavior*, and *PS: Politics and Political Science*. She also conducts research on racial and ethnic politics and is the author of *The Urban Voter: Group Conflict and Mayoral Voting in American Cities* (University of Michigan Press, 2004).

Harwood K. McClerking is assistant professor of political science at The Ohio State University. He has published in *Politics and Policy*, the *National Political Science Review, Political Psychology*, and the *Journal of Politics*. He has studied the representation of Black substantive policy issues in Congress, the effect that Black and White political leaders have on how citizens come to view events as racist, and how groups maintain identification among individual members through political means and everyday discourse.

Laura R. Olson is professor of political science at Clemson University. Recent books include (as coauthor) *Women with a Mission: Religion, Gender, and the Politics of Women Clergy* (University of Alabama Press, 2005), and *Religion and Politics in America: Faith, Culture, and Strategic Choices* (Westview, 2003); and (as coeditor) *Religious Interests in Community Conflict* (Baylor University Press, 2007), *The Encyclopedia of American Religion and Politics* (Facts on File, 2003), and *Christian Clergy in American Politics* (Johns Hopkins University Press, 2001).

Hector L. Ortiz is a doctoral student in Political Science at the Maxwell School of Citizenship and Public Affairs of Syracuse University. He is a McNair Fellow and the Political Science Intern Coordinator at Onondaga Community College. His research interests include aging, public policy, public opinion, and political participation.

Anand Edward Sokhey is a Ph.D. candidate and the senior fellow in the Program in Statistics and Methodology (PRISM) at The Ohio State University. His research has appeared in leading journals including the *American Journal of Political Science* and *Social Science Quarterly*. His research interests include voting behavior, public opinion, religion and politics, and methodology. He is particularly interested in the role that interpersonal communication plays in acquiring political knowledge, fostering political participation, and influencing candidate evaluations.

Jeffrey M. Stonecash is Maxwell Professor in the Department of Political Science at Syracuse University. Recent books include *The Emergence of State Government: Parties and New Jersey Politics, 1950-2000* (Fairleigh Dickinson University Press, 2002), *Diverging Parties* (Westview, 2002), *Political Polling* (Rowman and Littlefield, 2003), and *Parties Matter* (Lynne Rienner, 2006). He is now completing a book reassessing the incumbency effect.

1

"GAPOLOGY" AND THE 2004 PRESIDENTIAL VOTE

❧

JOHN C. GREEN
LAURA R. OLSON

All manner of political observers are fascinated by "gaps" in voting behavior. Whether it is the now-famous "gender gap," the newly discovered "religion gap," or the once-prominent "generation gap," sharp differences in voting behavior often emerge around commonplace demographic characteristics such as gender, worship attendance, and age. Such gaps are intrinsically interesting to students of politics because they represent a potent way to understand election results. Like batting averages in baseball, simple statistics often offer the power of language in describing the political world.

Thus, voting gaps have become touchstones for political journalists and their readers. Even more importantly, these gaps have become basic metrics used by political professionals—the pollsters, consultants, and campaign managers who conduct today's campaigns. Even political scientists find voting gaps fascinating, and an inspiration for research. Indeed, it is a rare election analysis that does not begin with a tabulation of the vote by various demographic categories.

Of course, most observers understand that such voting "gaps" represent oversimplifications of the complex reality of voting behavior. But it is precisely such complexity that makes "gapology" so attractive: it connects something of compelling importance (such as who was elected president) with some key facts of everyday life (people's most obvious personal characteristics). Voting gaps reveal how various groups of voters responded to the choices before them at the polls. In some cases, voters conceive of themselves as belonging to one social group or another; one might see oneself primarily as an African American, a southerner, or a Catholic, for example. Such identifications influence electoral decisions directly. In other cases, voters may not think of themselves as belonging to a social group—for example, being married or earning a lower income—but the common experiences and values associated with these characteristics also have an impact on the vote. Of course, the effects that social factors can have on the vote are mediated through partisanship, because demography is linked to identification with the Democratic or Republican Party (or with neither, in the case of Independents). The enduring political influence of demography is found in the social characteristics of the coalitions of people who traditionally support each major political party.

This book is designed to explore the most important demographic voting gaps in American politics today, with emphasis placed on the development of these patterns in recent times and the key explanations for their existence. Taken together, the chapters presented in this book demonstrate that twenty-first-century Americans are divided on a wide range of political fronts—but not in all areas. In fact, one of the most interesting aspects of gapology is the study of gaps that are now much smaller than they have been in the past. And for all their simplicity, even a cursory look at voting gaps reveals a more nuanced picture of American politics than common images such as the "red state, blue state" maps popular in the news media.[1] We aim to describe some of this complexity through a collection of observations by leading scholars on a range of voting gaps.

A good place to begin is with an overview of "gapology" in the 2004 presidential elections, using data from the National Election Pool (NEP), the national "exit poll." Like all surveys, the NEP has its limitations, but it also has its virtues. For one thing, it is very likely that the respondents to the exit poll actually cast ballots in the election. In addition, the number of individuals interviewed is quite large, allowing for the analysis of voting gaps with a high degree of confidence.[2]

"GAPOLOGY" AND THE 2004 PRESIDENTIAL VOTE

Table 1.1 presents evidence on nine voting gaps in the 2004 presidential election, using the 2004 NEP data. Each "gap" is calculated as the net percentage difference in the vote for George W. Bush between the two categories in question. The gaps are listed in descending order of magnitude, with the overall two-party division at the bottom of the table (in bold) and the overall distribution of each demographic group in the U.S. population in the far right-hand column (in italics).[3]

By far the largest of the voting gaps in 2004 was accounted for by race, or perhaps more accurately, **race and ethnicity**. George W. Bush obtained 58.7 percent of the White vote (which comprised 77.1 percent of the electorate), but just 27.6 percent of the non-White vote (22.9 percent of the electorate). Thus, the race gap was 31.1 percent, which is about ten times larger than the overall Bush–Kerry vote differential (which was a margin of 3 percent according to these data: 51.5 for Bush and 48.5 percent for Kerry).

TABLE 1.1 ELECTORAL GAPS AND THE 2004 TWO-PARTY PRESIDENTIAL VOTE

	% FOR GEORGE W. BUSH	% FOR JOHN F. KERRY	GAP IN BUSH VOTE	% OF ELECTORATE
Racial/Ethnic Gap				
White	58.7	41.3	**31.1**	77.1
Non-White	27.6	72.4		22.9
Marriage Gap				
Married	58.0	42.0	**17.0**	62.8
Not married	41.0	59.0		37.2
Worship Attendance Gap				
Weekly worship attendee	61.1	38.9	**16.8**	41.8
Less than weekly worship attendee	44.3	55.7		58.2
Income Gap				
>$50,000 a year	57.0	43.0	**12.3**	54.8
<$50,000 a year	44.7	55.3		45.2
Region Gap				
South, Midwest	55.2	44.8	**8.6**	57.2
Northeast, West	46.6	53.4		42.8
Place Gap				
Suburbs, rural areas	54.5	45.5	**8.6**	60.7
Large and small cities	46.9	53.1		39.3
Gender Gap				
Male	55.5	44.5	**7.3**	46.0
Female	48.2	51.8		54.0
Generation Gap				
40 or older	53.3	46.7	**4.4**	65.5
Younger than 40	48.9	51.1		34.5
Education Gap				
Some college or less	53.1	46.9	**3.2**	57.9
College degree or more	49.9	50.1		42.1
Republicans	93.6	6.4	**82.8**	37.1
Democrats	10.8	89.2		36.5
ALL	**51.5**	**48.5**	**3.0**	100.0

Source: Data from the 2004 National Election Pool.

Considering the difference between Whites and Blacks alone, the gap is nearly 48 percent, but the greater Republican vote among Latinos, Asians, and other non-Whites narrowed the gap a bit in 2004.

The second-largest of the voting gaps in 2004 was the **marriage gap**, or the difference in vote choice between married and unmarried people (including the never married, divorced, and widowed). At 17 percent, the marriage gap was a little more than half the size of the race and ethnicity gap. Bush received 58 percent of the ballots cast by married voters (who made up 62.8 percent of the electorate). Meanwhile, Kerry obtained 59 percent of ballots cast by unmarried voters (who made up 37.2 percent of the electorate.) Like race and ethnicity, marital status is a complicated phenomenon: the personal experiences of divorce, separation, and multiple marriages can all have an impact on how people view the political world (and thus the vote); so can the larger number of single, never married individuals as well as people in various kinds of domestic partnerships.

The third-largest gap in the 2004 presidential vote was the **worship attendance gap**. At 16.8 percent, this gap was a tiny bit smaller than the marriage gap, just a bit more than half the size of the race gap, and more than five times larger than the Bush–Kerry differential overall. Some three-fifths of those who reported attending religious services weekly or more often voted for Bush, and nearly as many of the less-than-weekly attendees voted for John Kerry. The worship attendance gap is closely related to race, but in a complicated way: weekly attendees include White evangelical Protestants (one of the strongest Republican constituencies) as well as Black Protestants, who are among the most loyal of Democrats. Indeed, the full range of religious variables, including both affiliation and attendance, produces very large gaps in the presidential vote. For example, the division between weekly attending White born-again Protestants and religiously unaffiliated voters was nearly 56 percentage points in 2004, rivaling the size of the electoral gap between Whites and Blacks.

The **class gap**, or as it is measured here, the income gap, was the fourth-largest voting gap in 2004. At 12.3 percent, it was about two-fifths the size of the race gap and a bit smaller than the marriage and worship attendance gap—and roughly four times bigger than the Bush–Kerry vote difference overall. Voters with incomes of $50,000 a year or more backed Bush with 57 percent of their ballots (about the same as White voters overall), while 55.3 percent of voters earning less than $50,000 a year voted for Kerry (about the same as less-than-weekly worship attendees). As is the case with other demographic factors, the simple income gap obscures the full effect of income on vote choice: 64.1 percent of voters with incomes of $200,000 or more (3.4 percent of the total) voted for Bush, and 63.6 percent of those earning less than $15,000 (8.3 percent of the electorate) voted for Kerry. Voters with incomes between $30,000 and $50,000 broke almost evenly between the major party candidates.

The **region** and **place gaps** come next, each at 8.6 percent. These two gaps were both almost three times the size of the overall Bush–Kerry vote differential. In a crude way, these geographic gaps represented the "red" and "blue" states—and in a slightly more sophisticated way, the "red" and "blue" *localities* within states. Of course, creating dichotomous geographic measures is more than a bit arbitrary: Bush carried the South quite handily, as well as a good bit of the Midwest, where there were many close statewide contests. Kerry won the Northeast and the West Coast, but lost the Mountain and Plains states, in some cases by small margins. Bush also carried the suburbs, exurbs, and "no urbs" (rural areas). Meanwhile, Kerry won the urban vote, especially in the largest cities. Presumably, places on the electoral map vary in the shade of red, blue, and purple in large part because of the kinds of people who live there. But region and place each have an independent impact on the vote because the distinctive cultures of specific communities provide an important context for voting decisions.

At last we come to the **gender gap**, which ranked seventh among the nine voting gaps at 7.3 percent. It is noteworthy that the gender gap was less than half the size of the religion gap in 2004. The major explanation for this result was Bush's success with women: he won nearly half of their votes. Meanwhile, Kerry failed to even up the score among men, losing that contest by a sizable seven percentage points. Part of the story regarding the gender gap was a spillover effect of the marriage gap, with 60 percent of married men voting to reelect the president while 62 percent of unmarried women voted to replace Bush. But gender can matter in elections precisely because it encompasses so many different aspects of the life experiences of both women and men.

The next-to-last gap in the 2004 presidential election was the **generation gap**. At only 4.4 percent, it was about a quarter the size of the religion gap and a third the size of the class gap. Voters over the age of 40 supported Bush on balance, while those under 40 were more likely to vote for Kerry. One reason for the small size of the generation gap is that age had a complex relationship to the 2004 vote. The very youngest voters (aged 18 to 24) went solidly for Kerry—but so did the very oldest voters (aged 75 and older). Bush did well among middle-aged voters, but there was a good bit of variation, with his strongest support coming from 60- to 64-year-olds. However, Bush very nearly lost the 50- to 59-year-old vote.

The smallest of the voting gaps in 2004 was the **education gap**. At 3.2 percent, this gap was about one-tenth the size of the race gap. Bush won among voters without a college degree, while the candidates broke even among those with college degrees and postgraduate education. This dichotomy masks a strong curvilinear relationship. Kerry won the postgraduate vote by ten percentage points and just edged Bush out among voters without high school diplomas. In contrast, Bush won small majorities among high school, trade school, and college graduates. As much as the other demographic factors discussed here, the generation and education gaps are related to other gaps. Age is related to worship attendance and gender, and education is related to social class and income. And age and education are themselves closely related, given the increasing level of educational achievement of each successive generation.

The final entries in Table 1.1 are the votes of self-identified Republicans and Democrats. Unlike the demographic gaps, these measures of partisanship do not include the entire electorate, with Independents excluded for ease of presentation. This exercise is a reminder that demography often influences the vote through partisanship as well as other political attitudes and identifications. In 2004, partisan differences in voting behavior were vast: 93.6 percent of self-identified Republicans voted for Bush and 89.2 percent of self-identified Democrats voted for Kerry. These figures produce a huge "party gap" of 82.8 percent, more than twice the size of the race and ethnicity gap and roughly ten times larger than the gender gap.

These figures show how polarized the electorate was in 2004, with Republicans and Democrats making up about equal shares of the electorate (37.1 and 36.5 percent, respectively). However, part of the power of partisanship comes from excluding Independent voters from our analysis. Independents were less numerous than Democrats and Republicans in the 2004 electorate, and they divided their ballots very evenly, with Kerry edging Bush by a margin of 51 percent to 49 percent, which almost exactly mirrors the overall margin of victory. Scholars have long seen partisanship as representing a different level of political influence than demography.[4] On the one hand, voters are typically White or Black, male or female, and young or old before they are Republicans or Democrats. On the other hand, identification with one of the major political parties is a direct predictor of the vote in presidential elections—and most other elections, for that matter. Put another way, partisanship is the most important way in which demographic differences become political differences and thus become relevant at the ballot box.

PIECING THE GAPS TOGETHER

The possible links among these demographic factors raises the question of whether each may have had an independent effect on the 2004 presidential vote. Although a full model of the vote is beyond the scope of this chapter, Table 1.2 offers a quick look at the independent effects of the demographic factors discussed above on the vote in 2004. In the table, results for each demographic factor by itself appear in the first column; results for each demographic factor plus partisanship appear in the second column.[5]

The results displayed in Table 1.2 are instructive. Looking at the first column, each and every one of the voting gaps, crude as it may be, is statistically significant in our analysis. These results strongly suggest that the demographic factors are not simply reflections of one another. Thus, race is not merely another way of measuring income, nor is marriage another version of gender.

TABLE 1.2   VOTER GAPS AND THE 2004 BUSH VOTE

	DEMOGRAPHY ONLY		DEMOGRAPHY PLUS PARTY	
	B	SIG.	B	SIG.
Racial/Ethnic gap	1.479	***	0.818	***
Worship attendance gap	0.780	***	0.615	***
Education gap	0.453	***	0.485	***
Income gap	0.436	***	0.354	***
Gender gap	0.399	***	0.216	**
Marriage gap	0.349	***	0.286	***
Region gap	0.320	***	0.373	***
Place gap	0.132	*	0.178	*
Generation gap	–0.119	*	0.144	0.086
Partisanship	N/A	N/A	2.299	***
(Constant)	–1.837	***	–6.019	***
Nagelkerke R-square	0.187		0.634	
% predicted correctly	66%		84%	

*** $p<0.001$; ** $p<0.01$; * $p<0.05$.

Source: Data from the 2004 National Election Pool.

These factors are related to one another, to be sure, but they exert *independent* effects on vote choice as well. All but one of the voting gaps retains the same direction of impact shown in Table 1.1. The exception to this rule is the generation gap: once the effects of all the voting gaps are taken into account, the generation gap reverses itself, so that voters under 40 years of age appear to have been more likely to vote for Bush. One reason for this change is the inclusion of the marriage gap in our model: young, unmarried voters strongly backed Kerry in 2004, while young married voters preferred Bush. If the marriage gap is excluded from the analysis, the generation gap is not statistically significant.

The magnitude of the effects shown in Table 1.2 largely parallels the size of the voting gaps presented in Table 1.1, with the race, religion, and class gaps retaining their high rankings. However, there are several important exceptions to the ordering of the voting gaps when all the gaps are taken into account. For example, the education gap moves slightly ahead of the class gap. This pattern makes some sense because education is a component of social class. In addition, the region and marriage gaps leapfrog the gender gap.

The second column in Table 1.2 includes party identification, which, as one might expect, dwarfs the impact of all the other voting gaps, generally reducing their impact on the Bush vote. But notice that all of the gaps remain statistically significant. (The only major change is that the generation gap reverses sign-again.) Thus, we see that, at least in this analysis, demography is not simply a reflection of partisanship—although many aspects of demography affect how Americans view the major political parties. It is worth noting that the order of the impact of the voting gaps on the Bush vote changes a little when partisanship is included: the region and gender gaps trade places in the list. Otherwise, the order remains the same.

THE PLAN OF THE BOOK

This simple overview analysis is designed to illuminate the popular and scholarly fascination with "gapology." But certainly there is much more to be known about causes, consequences, and changes with regard to voting gaps. It is to a further exploration that we now turn. The following chapters take up these voting gaps one at a time—presented in order of their relative size in Table 1.1—exploring their development, causes, and consequences in some detail.

Chapter 2 discusses the race and ethnicity gap, with a special emphasis on African Americans. Harwood McClerking shows that the race gap became large in the 1960s and has remained large since. Racial and ethnic group identity is central to the voting behavior of ethnic and racial minorities, a pattern that has been common throughout American history.

Chapter 3 turns to the marriage gap, which has grown in importance since the 1990s. The appearance of the marriage gap reflects major changes in family structure over the last two generations. As Amy Gershkoff shows, there has been a dramatic increase in households headed by unmarried people, including single adults, cohabiting partners, divorced and separated individuals, widows and widowers—and these changes have had significant political ramifications.

Chapter 4 explores the worship attendance gap, which emerged as politically significant in the 1990s. The worship attendance gap reflects the political importance of religion—and specifically the significance of religious practice and belief in recent times. Laura Olson and John Green explain that religious commitment has both replaced and reinforced the connection between religious affiliation and the vote.

In **Chapter 5** Hector Ortiz and Jeffrey Stonecash examine the class gap, placing a special emphasis on the political significance of income. Class differences have been a staple of presidential politics since at least the 1930s and remain important today. However, the nature of social class has changed in recent times, with powerful implications for party coalitions, including the rise of competition from cultural issues.

Chapter 6 describes voting gaps based on geography, including the region and place gaps. Geography has often played a major role in the vote, with the "red state-blue state" division of 2000 and 2004 elections being the most recent example. Regions and places make a nuanced and complex contribution to national politics. James Gimpel and Kimberly Karnes emphasize the political distinctiveness of people who live in rural areas as compared with those who live in cities.

Chapter 7 considers the gender gap, which became the subject of considerable interest in the 1990s. The size of the gender gap has varied, however, declining somewhat in the early twenty-first century. Karen Kaufmann shows that the causes and consequences of the gender gap are complex, reflecting the interplay of social circumstances and campaign issues.

Chapter 8 analyzes the generation gap, which came to attention in the 1960s, when the mantra of youth was "don't trust anyone over 30." The generation gap has become smaller and less salient since then, reflecting both the arrival of new generations and the aging of past generations. As a result, Anand Sokhey and Paul Djupe demonstrate that age has a complex impact on the vote.

Chapter 9 looks at the voting gaps from the perspective of political professionals, describing how pollsters, consultants, and campaign managers take demography into account to devise and implement a winning strategy at the polls. Anna Greenberg, a leading political strategist and pollster herself, describes and discusses traditional and new ways of targeting voting gaps.

NOTES

[1]However, as we will see, geographic voting gaps are important as well.

[2]NEP 2004 and 2006 Exit Polls conducted by Edison-Mitofsky Research. For more information on the methodology, see http://www.exit-poll.net/electionnight/MethodsStatementNationalFinal.pdf.

[3]For a look at gapology in the 2000 presidential election (measured in a slightly different fashion), see Rick Farmer and John C. Green, "A Contest of Surprises: The 2000 Election in the United States," in *The Elections of 2000*, ed. Mary K. Kirtz, Mark J. Kasoff, Rick Farmer, and John C. Green (Akron, OH: University of Akron Press, 2005).

[4]For example, see Angus Campbell, Phillip E. Converse, Warren E. Miller, and Donald E. Stokes, *The American Voter* (New York: Wiley, 1960).

[5]These results are the product of binary logistic regression with the Bush vote coded "1" and the Kerry vote "0." Each of the voting gaps is coded dichotomously as in Table 1.1. Partisanship is measured with a three-point scale (Democrat=1; Independent=2; Republican=3).

2

RACIAL AND ETHNIC GAPS

❧

HARWOOD K. MCCLERKING

In this chapter, I embark on a journey through the social science literature to understand why there are such sizable racial and ethnic electoral gaps in the United States today. This journey takes us through a short intellectual history of the study of groups in politics, an assessment of why groups matter in politics, and a specific look at African Americans' distinctive partisanship and voting behavior as an exemplar of the power of group politics. Using the African-American example, I hone in on how group-based dynamics affect electoral politics in the United States.

Our first order of business is to document that there is a substantial gap in presidential voting behavior and party identification between Black and White Americans. As Chapter 1 in this volume demonstrates, this Black–White gap is far more sizable than any other American electoral gap. Blacks tend to vote overwhelmingly for Democratic candidates for president, giving the Democrats 90 percent and 88 percent of their votes in the 2000 and 2004 presidential elections, respectively. And Blacks have supported Democratic presidential candidates overwhelmingly since 1964. According to political scientists Hanes Walton and Robert Smith, "As late as 1960 Richard Nixon . . . received about 20–25 percent of the black vote. This all changed in 1964 . . . [when] 94 percent or more of Blacks voted for Johnson and the Democratic party."[1] Walton and Smith further note that since the 1960s, "little has changed in black partisanship, with the Black vote in presidential elections since 1968 averaging 88 percent for the Democratic Party as compared to 43 percent among white voters."[2]

For African Americans, this distinctiveness in the voting booth also reflects distinctiveness in party identification. The aforementioned pattern in presidential voting behavior is a direct result of Black party identification, as

TABLE 2.1   PARTY IDENTIFICATION OF AFRICAN AMERICANS IN PRESIDENTIAL AND CONGRESSIONAL ELECTIONS, 1952–2000

PARTY IDENTIFICATION	PRESIDENTIAL ELECTIONS (ALL YEARS: 1952–2000)	CONGRESSIONAL ELECTIONS (ALL YEARS: 1954–1998)
Democrat	75%	77%
	(1837)	(1690)
Republican	10%	9%
	(241)	(190)
Independent	8%	9%
	(226)	(189)
Apolitical/Don't know	6%	6%
	(148)	(134)

Source: American National Election Studies Cumulative File (1952–2000).

roughly three in four Blacks (on average) have identified themselves as Democrats in poll after poll since 1952 (see Table 2.1).

As we see in Figure 2.1, there have been substantial differences between Black and White Americans' identification with the major political parties from the middle of the twentieth century and into the twenty-first (1952–2004). These two groups were actually quite comparable in their party identification as recently as the 1950s, but as noted above, that changed in the 1960s.[3] Since that decade, a gap of 30 percentage points or more has separated Blacks and Whites in terms of their propensity to identify with the Democratic Party.

FIGURE 2.1   PERCENT IDENTIFYING AS DEMOCRAT BY RACE, 1952–2004

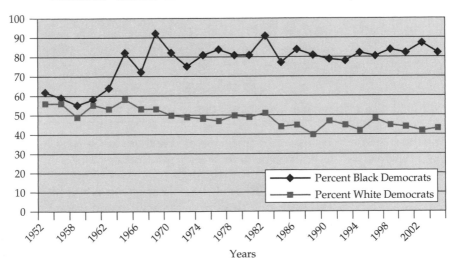

Years

TABLE 2.2   DEMOCRATIC VOTE IN PRESIDENTIAL ELECTIONS
BY RACE AND ETHNICITY, 1976–2004

	1976	1980	1984	1988	1992	1996	2000	2004
White	48	36	34	40	39	43	42	41
Black	83	83	91	89	83	84	90	88
Latino	82	56	66	70	61	72	62	53
Asian	N/A	N/A	N/A	N/A	41	46	55	56

Sources: 2000 data are from the Voter News Service Exit Poll as reported on
cnn.com/election/2000/epolls/us/poco.html; 2004 data are from the Edison
Media Research and Mitofsky Exit Poll as reported on cnn.com/election/
2004/pages/results/states/US/p/oo/epolls.o.html.

This gap is driven from both sides: African Americans have become more
Democratic; Whites, less Democratic.

These gaps in party identification also extend beyond African Americans
to include Latinos and Asian Americans, although both of these groups themselves often differ internally by country of national origin. Table 2.2 displays
the size of these voting gaps over time. Starting in 1976, it is clear that a majority of Latinos prefer the Democratic contender for the presidency. Although
Latino vote choice varies more than that of African Americans, Latinos are
much more likely to support Democratic candidates for president than are
White voters over this same time period. Due to small size in the overall population, reliable data on Asian-American voting behavior are difficult to obtain.
The first survey data presented here are from the 1992 presidential election.
In both 1992 and 1996, Asian-American voting patterns resemble those of
Whites more than those of Blacks and Latinos. However, this pattern changes
in 2000 and 2004. Beginning in 2000, a majority of Asian Americans support
the Democratic candidate, as do Blacks and Latinos. In short, the twenty-first
century thus far has witnessed a remarkable convergence in the voting behavior of non-White Americans.

GROUP IDENTIFICATION AND GROUP-BASED HEURISTICS

The bigger issue that lies before us is one of *why* there are such substantial
gaps between White Americans and members of other racial and ethnic
groups. Why is it that many members of ethnic minority groups are moving
toward the Democratic Party while a substantial number of Whites have been
moving away from the Democrats? The answer may lie in understanding how
group memberships and group identities affect the ways in which Americans
perceive the political world. From the earliest studies of voting behavior, scholars have noticed that group membership plays a powerful role in shaping
people's political attitudes and actions.

Americans' group memberships are politically relevant in several ways. Some individuals use their own membership in certain groups—or the group memberships of others—as reference points to coordinate their political opinions. Others may push this logic further and use more advanced group-based *heuristics*. A heuristic is a mental shortcut that people use to make sense of things about which they have limited information. The use of group memberships by individuals trying to make sense of politics is normal and widespread among Americans in general. Some members of various American racial and ethnic groups, such as African Americans, have developed group-based heuristics to make sense of how they should vote *as members of that group*. Some scholars have argued that such group-based heuristics are more politically salient than class differences for members of racial and ethnic minority groups, aggregating the individual members of such groups into solid supermajorities (60 percent or more) on one side of issues.[4] When you combine this possibility with the fact that party images seem to have become racialized (the Democratic Party is perceived as the pro-minority party while the Republican Party is perceived as less than helpful to minorities[5]), it makes sense that we would observe large racial and ethnic gaps in voting and party preference. The more developed the use of group-based heuristics among group members, the more distinctive—and "gappable"—the group becomes.

Some scholars also have noted why some Whites moved away from the Democrats. As the Democratic Party came to be identified with the progress of the civil rights movement, some Whites, especially southerners, moved away from the Democrats and toward the Republican party.[6] During the civil rights era, the two parties diverged on racial issues, creating a swift change in partisanship for Whites "as Blacks moved into the Democratic Party, southern Whites moved out."[7] Moreover, "as late as 1960, native-born southern Whites were much more Democratic in their partisan affiliations than were Blacks [by 28 points]. . . . By 1968, just eight years later, this large difference had completely reversed [Blacks were by then 31 points more Democratic]."[8] Scholars also have considered the extent to which long-standing racial preferences may have affected this development and whether Whites were more affected by racial considerations or class-based appeals by the Republican Party.[9]

A HISTORY OF GROUPS IN POLITICS

The study of groups has been a long-standing emphasis within political science and other social sciences, and some early scholars argued that groups are the most basic unit of politics itself.[10] Later scholars emphasized the importance of groups to the political process, suggesting that individual voters are less important than groups in politics.[11] One of the first empirical analyses of the relevance of group membership to voting behavior was presented in a book by scholars at Columbia University entitled *The People's Choice*.[12] A major contribution of this work is the idea that social membership plays a powerful role in shaping individuals' political orientations: "a person thinks, politically, as he is, socially. Social characteristics determine political preference."[13] Using what they called an "index of political predisposition," the Columbia scholars noted the great predictive power of three specific things about the residents of Erie County, Ohio, in 1940: their socioeconomic status, their religion, and whether they lived in a city. "Of all rich Protestant farmers almost 75 percent voted Republican, whereas 90 percent of the Catholic laborers living in Sandusky voted Democratic."[14]

The Columbia scholars continued their work on the political significance of group membership in a later book entitled *Voting: A Study of Opinion Formation in a Presidential Campaign*, an extensive study of the citizens of Elmira, New York, during the 1948 election cycle.[15] Here the Columbia scholars attempted to overcome some of the problems inherent in their first book. In particular, they worked to determine why vote choice fluctuated from election to election even though group membership tends to remain relatively steady, at least over the short term. One of the major ways in which the Columbia scholars worked to understand this seeming conundrum was by developing ideas about how political campaigns—and differential perceptions of campaigns—affect different groups in American society. They found that the higher an individual's social class (middle or upper class versus working or lower class), the more likely he or she would be to vote for the Republican candidate. Further, they found that Catholics who identify closely with their religion were more Democratic than more nominal Catholics. These findings and others led the Columbia scholars to argue that we can understand the political significance of groups through the concept of group identification. Those who identify strongly with any particular group are more likely to be affected politically by that group membership.

Scholars at the University of Michigan took the next step forward in the study of the political significance of group membership. They built on the work from the Columbia researchers by combining it with insights from social psychology. The Michigan scholars were able to create a larger and more generalizable set of theories because, instead of studying one county at a time (as did the Columbia scholars), they utilized random sample surveys of the entire American populace. The Michigan scholars' book, *The American Voter*, introduces what came to be known as the "Michigan Model" of voting.[16] This model illustrates the roles played by three key considerations when voters make their choices on election day: (a) long-term personal characteristics, especially party identification, (b) issue positions, and (c) candidate evaluations. Of these three concerns, party identification is considered to be the most important element, which is of great interest to group theory because party identification is nothing more than a form of group identification. The Michigan scholars note that in their theory and measurement, "the political party serves as the group toward which the individual may develop an identification, positive or negative, of some degree of intensity."[17]

One of the Michigan scholars, Philip Converse, later wrote a highly influential book chapter entitled "The Nature of Belief Systems in Mass Publics."[18] In this chapter, Converse examines the extent to which Americans tie themselves to ideological points of view. In Converse's view, democratic theory presupposes that citizens are able to make sense of the political world by arranging political opinions and beliefs on the left–right ideological scale (where liberalism is on the left and conservatism is on the right). The main point Converse makes is that people do *not* generally view the political world through predictable ideological frames. In fact, only 2.5 percent of the American population displays what Converse terms "ideological constraint," or perfectly predictable liberalism or conservatism across all political questions. Instead, Converse finds that most Americans made sense of politics through what they know about *reference groups*. He argues: "The Democratic Party might be disliked because 'it's trying to help the Negroes too much,' or the Republican Party might be endorsed because farm prices would be better with the Republicans in office [thereby benefiting farmers as a group]."[19]

Once the social science literature established that politically significant group identities are widespread among Americans, the question became one of understanding *why* group identification matters politically. Simply put, there are many ways in which individual citizens may appear to act more as a group than as individuals. It may just be that individual citizens share the same political views by chance, and this randomness accumulates in such a way that observers jump to the conclusion that like-minded citizens are acting as a group. On the other hand, it may be that a series of individuals react to similar political stimuli in the same way (think of a mass of people simultaneously raising umbrellas in response to an oncoming downpour).

Or there may be actual political coordination among individual citizens. Such coordination must be driven by homogeneity of experience, according to the Columbia scholars:

> How can we explain that social groups are politically homogeneous . . . ? There is, first, the fact that people who live together under similar external conditions are likely to develop similar needs and interests. They tend to see the world through the same colored glasses; they tend to apply to common experiences common interpretations. They will approve of a political candidate who has achieved success in their own walk of life; they will approve of programs [that] are couched in terms taken from their own occupations and adapted to the moral standards of the groups in which they have a common "belonging."[20]

Similarities in lived experience may lead to similarities in political outlook. But how can groups directly affect political behavior? The Columbia scholars note the rationale they perceive behind enduring group differences in political policy choices:

> In sum, the conditions underlying persistent voting cleavages seem to be (1) initial social differentiation such that the consequences of political policy are materially or symbolically different for different groups; (2) conditions of transmittibility from generation to generation; and (3) conditions of physical and social proximity providing for continued in-group contact in succeeding generations. In contemporary America, these conditions are best met in *class*, in *ethnic*, and in *ecological* divisions of the population. They continue to provide, then, the most durable social bases for political cleavage."[21]

Three key conditions may map policy views onto members of certain groups in an enduring fashion. First, the policy in question must matter to members of the group, either realistically or symbolically. Second, group members' policy preferences must cross generations. Third, continued proximity to group members must keep these preferences politically salient.

THE SIGNIFICANCE OF GROUPS IN POLITICS:
THE CASE OF AFRICAN AMERICANS

As noted above, African Americans are quite distinctive in their voting behavior and party identification. Why, however, is this so? There are several potential explanations. First, African Americans share a distinctive political culture and socialization pattern. Second, they receive politically relevant information from indigenous Black media, Black churches, and other predominantly Black organizations.[22] Political scientists Walton and Smith argue that the development and continuing strength of uniquely Black institutions is the core explanation of Black political distinctiveness.

Black institutions engender Black political distinctiveness in various ways. They emphasize the role of the *group* in comprehending the Black experience in the United States, both historically and presently. Specifically, Black institutions often stress group-oriented harms and remedies as opposed to those primarily affecting individuals. Emphasis is placed on the ways in which African Americans have been discriminated against *as a group* in the United States. This understanding extends to the study of Black voting. Walton and Smith use a Black institution-based critique of the prominence of individualistic models of political behavior.[23] Most models of voting behavior predict that voters will turn out to vote based on their *individual* access to resources, including education, income, and occupational prestige. In his earlier work, Walton argues that voting models miss a lot when they are constrained to individualistic conceptualizations alone, especially when it comes to Black voting.[24] He notes that individual-focused models of voting behavior fail to help scholars make sense of African-American voter registration patterns in the Deep South before and after the passage of the Voting Rights Act of 1965. Walton notes that in Louisiana on "January 1, 1897, 130,444 Blacks were registered. This number was approximately 44 percent of the total electorate. By March 17, 1900, only 5,320 Blacks were registered . . . 4.1 percent of the total electorate."[25] Models of voting that are based on individual-level participation cannot make sense of this fact. Nor can they help us understand why Black voter registration in Atlanta moved from "6,876 in February, 1946, to 21,137 in June, 1946, or the rise to 91,000 in 1969 from 63,000 in 1965."[26] The fact of the matter is that in Louisiana, a new state constitution designed to disenfranchise Blacks was instituted in 1898, and in Atlanta, federal courts overruled an anti-Black voter tactic, the exclusionary primary, in April 1946, leading directly to the upsurge in Black registration two months later. The surge in voting registration across the South after 1965 may be traced directly to the Voting Rights Act. These are all institutional, or what Walton calls "systemic," considerations that act on Blacks as a group, not as individuals.

There are other ways in which group memberships can, and do, impact individual voters. An example of such an impact is the political relevance of group-based resources. Political scientists Lucius Barker, Mack Jones, and Katherine Tate note that group-based resources play a highly significant role in equalizing Blacks' voting levels with those of Whites.[27] Such group-based resources include race consciousness and membership in indigenous Black organizations. "Race consciousness has been shown to promote Black political participation. Blacks' self-awareness as a discriminated and disadvantaged group leads them to be more politically active than other disadvantaged groups who lack a comparable collective identity."[28] An especially important indigenous institution for voting is the Black church.[29] In noting the difference between White and Black churches, Barker, Jones, and Tate say: "Although religious groups, such as those affiliated with the Christian Right, have recently become active in national politics, Black churches have traditionally been involved in politics."[30] Many argue that Black churches were instrumental in the Civil Rights Movement,[31] and Black churches still play an important role in facilitating the political participation of Blacks. Research shows that certain activities that tend to be distinctive to Black churches, such as inviting political candidates to speak to the assembled members, are associated with increased political participation among Blacks.[32]

How does the existence of uniquely Black institutions help us understand African Americans' recent preference for the Democratic Party? Walton and Smith note one way to understand why Blacks now vote so consistently for the Democrats: "Racial identification determines African American Democratic partisanship."[33] That may be so, but by what mechanism does this work? It is at this point that we must turn to the significance of group-based political heuristics among African Americans.

GROUP-BASED HEURISTICS AND AFRICAN-AMERICAN POLITICS

As noted earlier, heuristics are mental shortcuts that people use to make sense of things about which they have limited information. Sometimes these mental shortcuts rely on the groups to which one belongs as a reference point. A good bit of research has been undertaken on the political significance of group-based heuristics among African-Americans.[34] The work of political scientist Michael Dawson is particularly noteworthy in this regard. Dawson emphasizes a concept he calls "linked fate," which is the perception among individual African Americans that their individual fates are bound to that of African-Americans as a group. "The key to understanding the self-categorization process for African-Americans is the fact that the social category 'Black' in American society cuts across multiple boundaries."[35] Dawson argues that "linked fate" lies at the heart of what he terms the Black Utility Heuristic. The logic of this heuristic is that "as long as African Americans' life chances are powerfully shaped by their race, it is efficient for individual African Americans to use their perceptions of the interest of African Americans as a group, as a proxy for their own interest."[36] If individual Blacks are affected by how the world treats them due to their race, it makes a great deal of sense for African Americans to "substitute racial-group interests as a reasonable proxy for self-interest because information on racial-group interests was and is readily available and cheaper than information about one's own, unique situation."[37]

The claim here is that group identification and group-based heuristics built to accompany those racial-group identifications lead Blacks to support the Democrats. How does that work? Many observers of the political scene suggest that over the last four decades, the Democrats have offered more concrete benefits to Blacks as a group. The beginning of this policy phenomenon may be pinpointed in 1964:

> For one thing, Johnson's landslide [presidential election victory in 1964] had consequences for the Congress: a raft of liberal Democrats were brought in on Johnson's coattails, mainly replacing liberal Republicans. Starting in 1965, then, core support for racial liberalism, in the Senate and House alike, was to come from the Democratic Party. And for his part, the president continued to push civil rights hard. Johnson worked tirelessly for passage of the Voting Rights Bill of 1965 and the Fair Housing Bill of 1968; he established the Department of Housing and Urban Development with Robert Weaver as its head, the first Black cabinet member in U.S. history; he appointed Thurgood Marshall to the Supreme Court, the ninety-sixth justice and the first Black; he insisted on a proliferation of programs—VISTA, Head Start, Model Cities, the Office of Economic Opportunity, and more—designed to eradicate poverty and establish the Great Society. In all these conspicuous ways, Johnson succeeded in pushing and hauling the national Democratic Party to the left on matters of race.[38]

Studies of party imagery over time demonstrate that a majority of Americans perceive the Democrats as the party of the common person, the powerless, and the working class.[39] To be sure, the Democratic Party has worked hard in recent times to attract the electoral support of people who rank lower on the socioeconomic scale. We should not be surprised that many Blacks are attracted to the Democratic Party as individuals in light of the fact that many African Americans are not of high socioeconomic status. The dynamics of group identification add at least two elements to our expectations about the Democratic Party's ability to attract Black voters. First, most people do not pay much attention to politics, so it might be difficult for many Americans to know which party would be better for them individually. Black individuals who identify strongly with African Americans as a group, however, are rather likely to have access to this information about why Democrats might be better suited to represent them, thus matching lower-income Blacks with the more appropriate political party for them. Another—and perhaps controversial—way to apply the Black Utility Heuristic is the suggestion that Blacks whose individual economic interests might be better served by the Republican Party will nevertheless support the Democratic Party because they prioritize Blacks' *group* needs over their individual self-interest. This assertion suggests that as long as Black group identification remains politically salient, Blacks will resist class divisions and base their voting calculations on perceptions of which party favors Black interests *in general.*

MAKING SENSE OF HEURISTICS

Heuristics play a crucial role in helping Americans understand politics and reach conclusions about where they stand on issues and which candidates might be best suited to represent them. Since the publication of *The American Voter* in 1960, it has not been controversial to expect the vast majority of members of certain groups to support a particular party or candidate based on nothing more than that party's or candidate's group affiliation. Party identification is simply a form of group identification. It is a sense of belonging to, or feeling especially comfortable with, a particular political party. Logically, we expect individuals who strongly identify with groups that favor one party over the other to adopt that party identification themselves. Even though more and more Americans are identifying themselves as Independents these days, party identification still plays a powerful role in shaping voting behavior.[40] According to political scientist Larry Bartels: "This conventional wisdom regarding the 'decline of parties' is both exaggerated and outdated. . . . Far from 'partisans using their identifications less and less as a cue in voting behavior,' . . . 'partisan loyalties have as least as much impact on voting behavior at the presidential level in the 1980s as in the 1950s' . . . and even more in the 1990s than in the 1980s."[41]

Group-based heuristics aid voters' decision-making process in most simple, clearcut situations, but even heuristics cannot always clear up everything about politics. For example, how should strong Democrats and strong Republicans vote in primary elections when faced with a choice among candidates who all represent the same party? Preferring a Democrat is much more helpful when choosing between a Democratic and a Republican candidate than it is when asked to choose among several Democrats. Therefore, it may be useful to think about how group-based heuristics rely on clarity of choice. From the old argument that "voters are not fools,"[42] we learn that voting based on individual preferences depends on the available choices. For the logic of group-based preferences to apply, group members need to be provided with a clear sense of how each candidate might aid their group. The history of African Americans' relationship with the major political parties provides a good example of clear versus unclear choices. There was a 30-year period (from the 1930s until the 1960s) when neither of the major parties seemed to be doing much to help Blacks. During this time span, the African-American vote was in play, by default, for both parties. We have already noted that Blacks gave Nixon more support in 1960 than any Republican has received since then; Eisenhower also received roughly two-fifths of the Black vote in 1956.[43] This period in the mid-twentieth century, however, is considered abnormal. Walton and Smith note that, generally speaking, African Americans exhibit a "one party at a time" dynamic, wherein only one party takes the chance of offering policies that Blacks would find attractive. In this context they cite the famous late-nineteenth-century statement by Frederick Douglass that the "Republican party is the deck, all else the sea" to argue that Blacks perceived radical Republicans as their best choice because they were their *only* choice at that time.[44] If one party is perceived to be hostile to Black concerns (as were the Democrats in the late nineteenth and early twentieth centuries), the other party has to do very little to capture the Black vote. This is a major concern today, as many observers wonder whether the Democratic Party is still working hard enough to attract the Black vote with actual policy; instead, it may merely be claiming its status as the "deck" of the twenty-first century. Barker, Jones, and Tate argue that Blacks have such extreme interests on the left–right dimension that only left-of-center political parties will hold appeal for them.[45] The Republicans of the immediate post–Civil War era were left-of-center, as have been the Democrats since the 1960s. This is in large part why the party preferred by Blacks has fluctuated over the long term.

EXPECTATIONS ON THE FUTURE OF RACIAL/ETHNIC ELECTORAL GAPS

We have established that African Americans have a very distinctive, group-based approach to politics. We also have established that this distinctiveness flows in large part from the existence of uniquely Black institutions. In which political directions should we expect African Americans to move in the future?

As we noted earlier, the Black–White electoral gap is two-sided. Blacks are tightly tied to the Democratic Party, but Whites meanwhile are pulled toward the Republican Party in ever-greater numbers. Even racially liberal Whites have been moving in a more Republican direction in recent years,[46] just as members of all racial and ethnic minority groups seem to be moving toward the Democrats. This suggests that the racial and ethnic electoral gap will continue to grow or at least remain steady for a while.

What can we expect in the voting behavior and party preferences of African-Americans in the near term? African-American group identity and group identification continues to be robust, even in the face of advancing class diversity among group members.[47] Thus, we should expect to see the basic structure of Black political behavior remain relatively steady, at least in the short run. When choices are clear, those Blacks who feel a strong attachment to African Americans as a group will make political decisions primarily by considering the needs of the group. On the other hand, cross-cutting issues constitute a major unknown about the future of Black voting. The Black political agenda traditionally has concentrated on "consensus" issues: issues that are framed as being important to every member of a group.[48] Several issues come together to constitute the "Post–Civil Rights Era Black Agenda": full employment, guaranteed income, comprehensive national health insurance, and increased federal funding for elementary, secondary, and higher education.[49] Cross-cutting issues, on the other hand, are concerns that disproportionately and directly affect only *certain segments* of a marginal group, such as Black gays and lesbians.[50] Some of the most powerful cross-cutting issues today deal with religiosity and the root of social problems in the Black community. As many observers have noted, the Black church is one of the cornerstones of the Black community, and belief in the centrality of the church is an important aspect of Black social and political distinctiveness.[51] As such, it seems likely that the ownership of religious and moral issues that the Republican Party recently has asserted might eventually heighten political divisions within the African-American community. Black people are, on the whole, quite religious—and quite conservative in their theology. For now, race trumps religion in American politics. Whether this will continue to be true in the future, however, remains to be seen.

NOTES

[1]Hanes Walton and Robert Smith, *American Politics and African American Quest for Universal Freedom* (New York: Pearson Longman, 2006): 129.
[2]Ibid.
[3]Walton and Smith (2006), passim.
[4]Michael Dawson, *Behind the Mule: Race and Class in African-American Politics* (Princeton, NJ: Princeton University Press, 1994).
[5]Donald Kinder and Lynn Sanders, *Divided by Color: Racial Politics and Democratic Ideals* (Chicago: University of Chicago Press, 1996).

[6]See Edward Carmines and James Stimson, *Issue Evolution: Race and the Transformation of American Politics* (Princeton, NJ: Princeton University Press, 1989); Michael W. Giles and Kaenan Hertz, "Racial Threat and Partisan Identification," *American Political Science Review* 88 (1994): 317–326. Keith T. Poole and Howard L. Rosenthal, *Ideology and Congress* (New Brunswick, NJ: Transaction, 2007).

[7]Kinder and Sanders (1996): 217; see also Poole and Rosenthal (2007).

[8]Kinder and Sanders (1996): 217–218.

[9]See, for example, Mark D. Brewer and Jeffrey M. Stonecash, "Class, Race Issues, and Declining White Support for the Democratic Party in the South," *Political Behavior* 23 (2001): 131–155.

[10]Arthur Bentley, *The Process of Government: A Study of Social Pressures* (Chicago: University of Chicago Press, 1908).

[11]See Robert A. Dahl, *A Preface to Democratic Theory* (Chicago: University of Chicago Press, 1956); David B. Truman, *The Governmental Process: Political Interests and Public Opinion* (New York: Knopf, 1951).

[12]Paul F. Lazarsfeld, Bernard Berelson, and Helen Gaudet, *The People's Choice* (New York: Columbia University Press, 1944).

[13]Ibid., 27.

[14]Ibid., 26.

[15]Bernard Berelson, Paul F. Lazarfeld, and William McPhee, *Voting: A Study of Opinion Formation in a Presidential Campaign* (Chicago: University of Chicago Press, 1954).

[16]Angus Campbell, Phillip E. Converse, Warren E. Miller, and Donald E. Stokes, *The American Voter* (New York: Wiley, 1960).

[17]Ibid., 122.

[18]Philip E. Converse, "The Nature of Belief Systems in Mass Publics," in *Ideology and Discontent*, ed. David E. Apter (New York: Free Press, 1964).

[19]Ibid., 216.

[20]Lazarsfeld, Berelson, and Gaudet (1944): 148–149.

[21]Berelson, Lazarsfeld, and McPhee (1954): 75. Emphasis in original. By "ecological," the authors refer to "the ecological division of region or size of community (e.g., the metropolitan area as against the small town)": 73.

[22]Walton and Smith (2006).

[23]Ibid.

[24]Hanes Walton, *Invisible Politics: Black Political Behavior* (Albany: State University of New York Press, 1985).

[25]Ibid., 86.

[26]Ibid.

[27]Barker, Jones, and Tate (1999), 86.

[28]Ibid., 238.

[29]Fredrick C. Harris, *Something Within: Religion in African-American Political Activism* (New York: Oxford University Press, 1999); C. Eric Lincoln and Lawrence H. Mamiya, *The Black Church in the African-American Experience* (Durham, NC: Duke University Press, 1990).

[30]Ibid. See also Harris (1999).

[31]See Aldon D. Morris, *The Origins of the Civil Rights Movement* (New York: Free Press, 1984).

[32]Harwood McClerking and Eric McDaniel, "Belonging and Doing: Political Churches and Black Political Participation," *Political Psychology* 26 (2005): 721–734.

[33]Walton and Smith (2006): 132.

[34]Dawson (1994).

[35]Ibid., 76.

[36]Ibid., 61.

[37]Michael Dawson, *Black Visions: The Roots of Contemporary African American Political Ideologies* (Chicago: University of Chicago Press, 2001): xi.

[38]Kinder and Sanders (1994): 206–207.

[39]Tasha S. Philpot, *Race, Republicans, and the Return of the Party of Lincoln* (Ann Arbor: University of Michigan Press, 2007).

[40]Bruce E. Keith, David B. Magleby, Candice J. Nelson, Elizabeth Orr, Mark C. Westlye, and Raymond E. Wolfinger, *The Myth of the Independent Voter* (Berkeley: University of California Press, 1992); Warren E. Miller and J. Merrill Shanks, *The New American Voter* (Cambridge, MA: Harvard University Press, 1996).

[41]Larry M. Bartels, "Partisanship and Voting Behavior, 1952–1996," *American Journal of Political Science* 44 (2000): 35.

[42]V. O. Key, *The Responsible Electorate* (Cambridge, MA: Belknap Press of Harvard University Press, 1966).

[43]Barker, Jones, and Tate (1999): 218.

[44]Walton and Smith (2006): 145.

[45]Barker, Jones, and Tate (1999): 223.

[46]Philpot (2007).

[47]Dawson (1994); McClerking (2001).

[48]Cathy Cohen, *The Boundaries of Blackness: AIDS and the Breakdown of Black Politics* (Chicago: University of Chicago Press, 1999).

[49]Walton and Smith (2006): 113.

[50]Cohen (1999).

[51]Harris (1999).

3

THE MARRIAGE GAP

❖

AMY R. GERSHKOFF

According to the 2004 exit polls, married people preferred George W. Bush by a 15-point margin, while unmarried people chose John Kerry by 18 points. This "marriage gap" in 2004 was striking but not unusual. Over the last several elections, married Americans have formed a key part of the Republican base, while unmarried Americans—those who are single, separated, divorced, or widowed—have comprised a cornerstone of the Democratic Party's base. The resulting gap in the voting behavior of married and unmarried Americans increasingly has become a consequential feature of American politics.[1]

The marriage gap also extends beyond the vote. Married and unmarried voters differ substantially in terms of party identification, ideology, and positions on a range of issues including the economy, welfare, health care, and moral values. Perhaps because these two groups of Americans have such different lifestyles, they have come to expect different types and levels of services from the government.

Interestingly, the marriage gap has been relatively understudied compared to other electoral gaps, despite the fact that in 2004 it was second in size only to the race/ethnicity gap. Moreover, in spite of the fact that the gap is growing with each passing election, relatively little is known about the causes and consequences of the marriage gap in American politics.

This chapter explores the marriage gap, its potential origins, and its consequences for American politics. I begin by documenting the gap between married and unmarried America in terms of partisanship, ideology, and values. Next, I discuss the rise of "unmarried America," how demographic shifts have contributed to changing the face of the American family, and the consequences of these shifts for the politics of the marriage gap. Drawing on existing literature on the topic, I turn to possible structural explanations of the marriage gap and offer a new explanation that merits further study. I conclude by discussing the future of the marriage gap and its implications for American politics.

THE DIFFERENT POLITICAL WORLDS OF MARRIED
AND UNMARRIED AMERICA

In all but four of the last 14 presidential elections, married Americans have voted for the Republican candidate by a substantial margin. And in half of these elections, including every election since 1984, unmarried voters gave Democratic candidates a substantial edge. Thus, as Figures 3.1 and 3.2 demonstrate, the marriage gap has been a long-standing phenomenon in American politics, despite the fact that it has only recently begun to receive scholarly attention.

In fact, the marriage gap extends beyond the presidential vote to congressional voting behavior as well, and this pattern has become even more prominent in recent years. Examining the 2004 U.S. Census data, Dennis Cauchon reported that in the 109th Congress, "Republicans control[led] 49 of the 50 districts with the highest marriage rates. Democrats control[led] all 50 districts with the lowest marriage rates."[2] Married people evidently prefer Republican candidates in general, whereas unmarried people prefer Democrats.

Unsurprisingly, the marriage gap extends to party identification itself. In 1988, 51 percent of unmarried American adults either identified with or said they usually lean toward the Democratic Party. Only 36 percent considered themselves Republicans or Republican leaners, creating a 15-point gap in party identification. By 1996, that gap in partisanship had grown to 27 points, and it has held steady in the last several elections. In short, as Figure 3.3 shows, unmarried Americans are Democratic base supporters.

FIGURE 3.1   PRESIDENTIAL VOTE OVER TIME: MARRIED

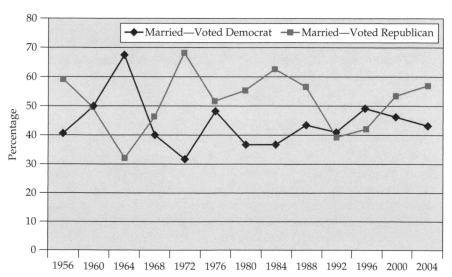

FIGURE 3.2   PRESIDENTIAL VOTE OVER TIME: UNMARRIED

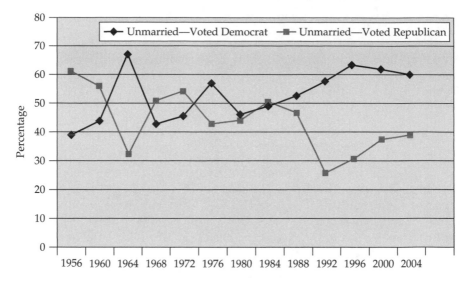

Since 1992, unmarried Americans have supported Democratic presidential candidates over their Republican opponents by a minimum of a 12-point margin, and have self-identified as Democrats by more than a 24-point margin. The fact that unmarried Americans are fairly uniform in their support for

FIGURE 3.3   PARTY IDENTIFICATION FOR UNMARRIED ADULTS OVER TIME

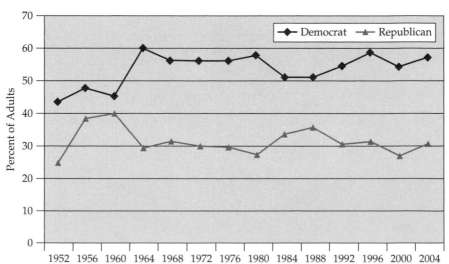

the Democratic Party is all the more striking given their demographic diversity: unmarried America encompasses people of both genders from every race and ethnic group. Unmarried people vary widely in income, education, and occupation. They are scattered about the country and live in rural, suburban, and urban areas. They even vary in the reasons why they are unmarried, as this category encompasses people who are separated, widowed, divorced, and never married. In contrast to unmarried Americans' strong support for the Democratic Party, Figure 3.4 shows that married adults' partisan identification has fluctuated in the last two decades, first creating a Democratic advantage, then a Republican advantage, then a Democratic advantage, and so forth.

Despite all of the evidence, there is no universal agreement about the existence of the marriage gap. Most scholars who have analyzed the marriage gap have found marital status to be a powerful predictor of vote choice,[3] but other scholarship has found that the effects of marriage on the vote disappear when other variables, such as gender, income, race, and education, are included as controls.[4] Still other scholars have found evidence to support both of these competing claims.[5] Journalists and practitioners on the whole appear convinced that marriage has at least a modest, and perhaps a major, effect on vote choice.[6] Much of the scholarly disagreement appears to be about the origins of the marriage gap. What factors might account for the emergence of a marriage gap among American voters?

FIGURE 3.4   PARTY IDENTIFICATION AMONG MARRIED ADULTS OVER TIME

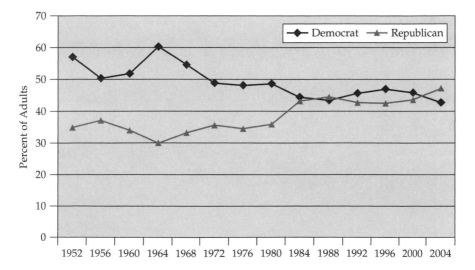

THE RISE OF UNMARRIED AMERICA AND THE CHANGING AMERICAN FAMILY

In the early part of the twentieth century, the average American family looked much like families portrayed in Victorian art and literature. By far the most common portrait of the American family was one of two married, heterosexual parents whose children lived at home until they themselves married, moved out, and established their own two-heterosexual-parent households. Young people rarely lived by themselves before getting married. Divorce rates in those days were extremely low, so there were few people living on their own after being married, save widows and widowers. Moreover, life expectancies were lower in the earlier part of the twentieth century, so the number of widows and widowers was small by contemporary standards.[7]

Today, the portrait of the typical American family is quite different. In fact, there is no "average" family. Modern "families" include a wide range of single people, including never-married men and women living on their own, often into their forties or throughout their entire lives; homosexual couples; heterosexual couples cohabitating but not marrying; single parents; divorced people; and widows and widowers, some of whom have remarried, some of whom have not.[8] And the number of Americans who fall into the unmarried category has grown steadily since 1960 (see Figure 3.5). Whereas in the early twentieth century many of these living arrangements would have raised more

FIGURE 3.5   PERCENTAGE OF AMERICANS AGED 15+ WHO ARE UNMARRIED

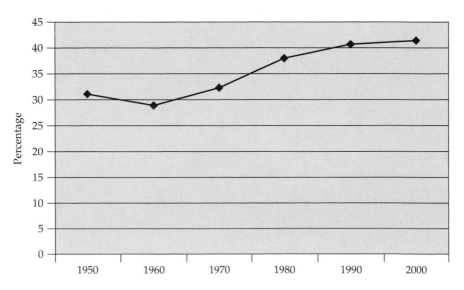

than one eyebrow, today all of these family arrangements have become commonplace in American society. All of these trends contribute to a rise in unmarried America: today, an unmarried man or woman heads nearly half of all households.[9]

Of the many trends that explain the growth of the unmarried sector of the American population, the two most important factors are (1) the rise in divorce rates and (2) the increasing proportion of young people delaying marriage. Both trends developed simultaneously, beginning slowly in the middle part of the twentieth century, and escalating rapidly since 1960.[10]

Divorce rates have climbed precipitously since Victorian times. In 1900, less than one-half of one percent of all males and one-half of one percent of females were divorced, but by 2004, 8.6 percent of males and 11.5 percent of females were divorced (see Figure 3.6).[11] Changes in divorce laws, including the introduction of "no-fault" divorce as a legally permissible and defensible concept, contributed to the rise in divorce rates, as did basic changes in American social norms.[12]

Delaying marriage is less a consequence of the legal infrastructure than it is a result of changes in economics, education, and social norms, particularly with regard to women. The last century has seen a dramatic rise in education rates among women[13] that has been coupled with changing norms about women in the workforce.[14] As women as a group grew better educated and it became more socially acceptable for them to seek employment in skilled jobs, they became more financially independent. Thus, marriage became one of many available paths—as opposed to the only path—available for women

FIGURE 3.6   DIVORCE RATE BY GENDER OVER TIME

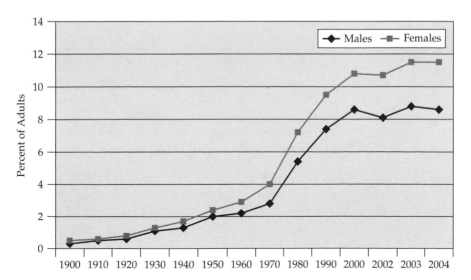

seeking to ensure their financial security. Meanwhile, education rates also increased among men.[15] As going away to college increasingly became a norm among young people of both genders, many delayed marriage until the completion of their education.[16]

Social norms changed too, making living alone much more socially acceptable, in addition to being economically feasible. The sexual revolution that began in the 1960s and continued through the rest of the century made it more socially acceptable for people to have intimate relationships as unmarried adults. In particular, the advent of oral contraceptives in the 1960s is widely credited in both the popular press and the academic literature for contributing to the depression of marriage rates in subsequent decades.[17]

Changing norms regarding family living arrangements are evident in the popular television series of different decades. In the 1950s, series such as *Leave It to Beaver* glorified traditional married life. By the 1970s, series such as *The Brady Bunch* (featuring a blended family resulting from second marriages) continued to place the spotlight on marriage and children, but suggested as well that multiple models of family could be acceptable. By the 1990s, such series had been replaced with the likes of *Friends* and *Sex and the City*, which glorified the single life. Living alone went from being the mark of a social pariah to evidence of independence and self-reliance.[18] Such changes in the culture made it not only possible but even probable that young people would delay marriage, as Figure 3.7 shows.

FIGURE 3.7   MEDIAN AGE AT FIRST MARRIAGE BY GENDER OVER TIME

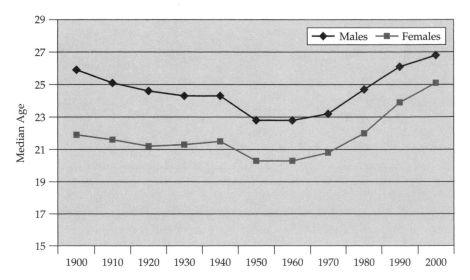

A TALE OF TWO COHORTS

Since the early 1990s, married and unmarried Americans have formed two remarkably cohesive groupings, despite vast differences within each group in terms of age, education, income, race, and gender. This diversity is particularly noteworthy among the unmarried, because again this grouping includes those who are unmarried for a variety of reasons: single, separated, divorced, or widowed. Yet, despite the variegated set of reasons for their marital status, unmarried people share the common experience of being on their own—financially, emotionally, and personally.

The financial component of being single is particularly striking. Today, 35 percent of unmarried adults have annual household incomes of less than $30,000 per year, compared to just 17 percent of married adults with household incomes of less than $30,000 per year.[19] Thus, many more unmarried people live on the edge financially, which undoubtedly contributes to their more liberal attitudes on social welfare programs and other government-sponsored economic assistance.[20] Married people not only have a potential second source of income (their spouse), but they also have a potential second source of health insurance, child care, and other important kinds of support.

Married and unmarried people also differ in their geographic mobility. Unmarried people tend to be much more mobile, moving much more frequently.[21] This fact has important political implications: the more often a person moves, the less likely he or she is to re-register to vote and to be contacted by political parties and candidates. Thus, unmarried people are much less likely than their married counterparts to be contacted by parties, candidates, or interest groups.

CAUSES OF THE MARRIAGE GAP

But why would these demographic differences matter politically, creating a marriage gap at the polls with the potential to trump other demographic variables in predicting vote choice? What follows is a survey and critique of the most common explanations of the marriage gap, followed by a discussion of a new cause—party outreach—that has not been part of previous studies of the marriage gap.

In the scholarly literature, the causes of the marriage gap center primarily on economics and values. Again, unmarried Americans are on their own financially and therefore much less likely to be financially secure relative to their married counterparts. This relative lack of financial security means that unmarried people seek different economic policies from the government than do married people, as reflected in their greater support of welfare policy.[22] Given that Democrats traditionally have been the party advocating for government-sponsored economic assistance, it is thus unsurprising to discover that unmarried Americans are so loyal to the Democratic Party. By contrast, married Americans are much better off financially. Therefore, they are much more likely to be concerned about lowering taxes than about maintaining welfare programs; hence their policy preferences much more closely align with those of the Republican Party.[23] Thus, one argument about the underlying cause of the marriage gap is that the differing financial circumstances of unmarried and married Americans lead to disparate economic policy views among voters in the two cohorts, which in turn leads to differential levels of support for the two parties, respectively. This argument has been advanced by multiple scholars.[24]

Evidence for this argument centers on well-documented differences in attitudes about economic issues—particularly with regard to social welfare issues—between married and unmarried voters. Most recently, for instance, in the 2006 Democracy Corps post-election survey of those who reported voting in the midterm congressional elections, two-thirds of unmarried respondents said they agreed with the statement that "the government should play a vital role ensuring all individuals have the same opportunity to succeed," while less than half of married respondents agreed with that statement. Similarly, only 29 percent of unmarried respondents said that they agreed with the statement "the government should stop providing social services and give people the tools to make their own choices on important issues." In contrast, almost half of married respondents agreed with that statement. Other Democracy Corps surveys of likely voters taken throughout 2006 obtained a similar result.

As an additional check on the Democracy Corps data, and in order to ensure that these differences in attitudes are present not just in likely voters but also with adults more generally (including those who do not vote), I examined attitudes about social welfare among the married and unmarried cohorts using American National Election Studies (ANES) data. ANES includes a question about whether the government should devote more resources to social services. The question was asked every two years from 1982 to 2004. The ANES data reveal that unmarried adults consistently are much more supportive of government services relative to their married counterparts, while married persons favor lower taxes at the expense of government services. The 2004 data appear in Figure 3.8. Data from other years reveal a similar gap in the economic preferences of married and unmarried adults.

The marriage gap almost certainly has economic underpinnings. However, economics alone cannot fully explain the marriage gap, for it presumes that at the moment never-married men and women get married, their economic values change entirely, which clearly seems implausible. To be sure, once a person becomes married, he or she has, potentially, additional income and financial security, which could over time gradually alter the value he or she places on the government-sponsored safety net. Nevertheless, it seems implausible that an unmarried person would change his or her views so dramatically

FIGURE 3.8   SUPPORT FOR GOVERNMENT SERVICES AND SPENDING
AMONG UNMARRIED ADULTS

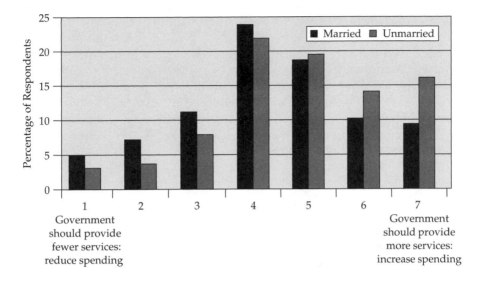

virtually overnight, moving from a Democratic to a Republican loyalist as soon
as he or she says, "I do."

Another oft-cited explanation for the marriage gap centers on moral values. Generally speaking, married people have more conservative views than
their unmarried counterparts on "values" issues such as abortion and same-sex
marriage. As the argument goes, being part of a "traditional" family structure
makes married people less inclined to be accepting of "non-traditional" family structures.[25] Data bear this argument out. Returning to the 2006 Democracy
Corps post-election survey of voters, 55 percent of unmarried voters said that
"homosexuality is a way of life that should be accepted by society," while less
than half of married people agreed with that statement. In addition, more than
half of unmarried voters registered cool feelings toward "pro-life, anti-abortion
groups," compared to only 43 percent of married voters.

ANES data show a similar pattern across the last several decades. Support
for abortion has declined in general in the last several years. In 1992, 45 percent
of Americans said, "by law, a woman should always be able to obtain an abortion as a matter of personal choice." By 2004, only 31 percent of adults agreed
with that statement. Nevertheless, support for abortion rights has been consistently higher among unmarried adults relative to their married counterparts. In
2000, for instance, 44 percent of unmarried adults believed that a woman should
be able to obtain an abortion as a matter of personal choice, while only 36 percent of married adults agreed; in 2004, 33 percent of unmarried adults agreed,
compared to fewer than three in ten married adults.

As with economic explanations, while values almost certainly explain part of the marriage gap, this explanation fails to account fully for the gap in vote choice between married and unmarried persons. It cannot be the case that upon marriage, the single person forgets his or her unmarried past and suddenly becomes disapproving toward same-sex couples and opposed to abortion. Similarly, a once-married woman who gets divorced or becomes widowed assuredly cannot overnight alter her views on important moral issues simply because her marriage dissolved.

Thus, to explain the marriage gap, we need to include at least one other variable in the equation, one that actually can change overnight as one moves from unmarried to married or married to unmarried. That variable is political mobilization.

POLITICAL MOBILIZATION

I hypothesize that the marriage gap in the American electorate is due, at least in part, to differential rates of political mobilization. If Democrats contact unmarried persons more frequently than do Republicans, and if Republicans contact married persons more often than do Democrats, then the preexisting political disparity between married and unmarried persons (in terms of partisanship, ideology, and issue positions) is exacerbated by a gap in where the two political parties are spending their resources.

To examine this possibility, I again used ANES data. ANES asks respondents whether they have been contacted by one of the major parties during the campaign, and if so, which party contacted them. These questions have appeared in every presidential election year survey since 1956, which means we have time series data on this phenomenon. The question wording varied slightly over time, but consistently the key word ANES used was "contact." Presumably, "contact" could include mail, telephone, e-mail, face-to-face visits, and so forth.

The data show that unmarried persons are contacted far less often by *either* political party than their married counterparts. In 2004, for instance, 43 percent of married adults recalled receiving communication from at least one of the major parties, compared to only 30 percent of unmarried adults. In midterm election years, the contact gap is even larger, with 43 percent of married people recalling receiving communication from at least one of the major parties, but only 22 percent of unmarried people recalling being contacted. This result makes sense in light of unmarried voter's higher levels of geographic mobility. Although these survey questions inherently are potentially subject to respondent over-reporting, there is no reason to believe that married people would be more likely than unmarried people to over-report being contacted by a political party.

Figure 3.9 allows us to examine political mobilization by the two major parties. The figure provides mixed evidence for the hypothesis posited above.

FIGURE 3.9 PARTY MOBILIZATION BY MARITAL STATUS

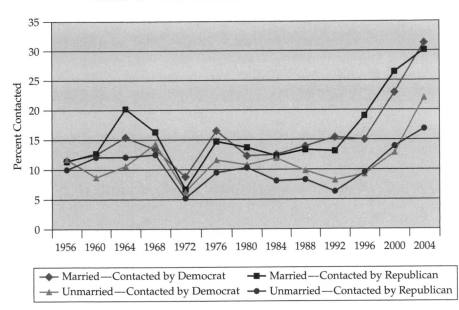

Both parties seem to contact both married adults and unmarried adults at roughly the same rates, although married adults are contacted much more often than their unmarried counterparts. In 1996 and 2000, married people were more likely to be contacted by Republicans than by Democrats. In 1996, however, married people were more likely to vote for Bill Clinton than Bob Dole, closing the marriage gap at least temporarily. On average, unmarried people are slightly more likely to be contacted by the Democratic Party than by the Republican Party, but in 1996 and 2000, unmarried adults actually were more likely to be contacted by the Republicans than by the Democrats. Only in 2004 did Democrats "out-mobilize" unmarried voters relative to the Republicans.

On their own, these data provide only mixed support for the political mobilization hypothesis. However, there are several reasons to be cautious in interpreting Figure 3.9. First, the data used are *self-reports* of voter contact, which may differ—perhaps substantially—from what actually occurred. Furthermore, in modern campaigns, it is often difficult to tell which party is actually communicating with voters, as issue advocacy organizations and 527 committees often send mail and make phone calls that clearly advantage a particular party even though the sponsoring organizations themselves are not explicitly partisan, creating error in the party attribution of the self-reports.

We can use the ANES panel studies to examine whether it may be the case that when an unmarried person gets married or a married person becomes separated, widowed, or divorced, he or she begins to receive different communications from the two parties. In order to examine this possibility, I used two ANES panel studies: 1992–1997 and 2000–2004. Because there were so few people whose marital status changed during either of these time frames, I jointly examined anyone who changed marital status in either time frame. This method of analysis is not ideal, because I am combining data collected during two different time frames. During these two time frames, parties and campaigns had different resources and contact strategies. At the same time, this strategy gives me enough cases to be able to examine how mobilization changes when marital status changes. In order to use as many cases as possible, I include adults from both samples who changed marital status, and not merely those who were eligible, registered, or likely voters.

Altogether there were 84 respondents who were unmarried at the beginning of one of the panels and were married by the end of the panel. The data show that *neither* political party contacted 72 of the 84 respondents (86 percent) at the beginning of their panel (when they were unmarried). Among those 72 respondents who were not contacted in the first year of the panel study, 21 (30 percent) were subsequently contacted by one of the parties after their marital status changed to married. Of those, the Republican Party contacted 19 and the Democratic Party contacted 11.

By contrast, among those who were unmarried throughout the entire panel (300 respondents), there were 259 (86 percent) who were not contacted in the first year of the study. Of those, 68 (26 percent) were contacted by one of the two parties in the second year of the study. Among those who were contacted the second year but not the first, two-thirds were contacted by the Democratic Party while only half were contacted by the Republican Party.

Overall, the data suggest that individuals who got married over the course of the study's time frame may have modestly improved their chances of being contacted by one of the parties, although the sample size is too small to reach this conclusion definitively. Moreover, when individuals were contacted post-marriage, it appears that they were more likely to have been contacted by the Republicans than by the Democrats, although again our sample size is too small to draw any concrete conclusions. I encourage other scholars to replicate this result using future panel studies.

Among respondents whose marital status changed during the panel, recall that only 12 were contacted by either of the major parties in the first year of the panel study (72 of 84 were not contacted). In the last year of the panel study, after their marital status had changed, only four of these respondents reported being contacted by either major party, so eight were no longer contacted after getting married. Again, the small sample size makes final conclusions impossible.

Readers may wonder about those who were married in the first year of the panel but were separated, widowed, or divorced by the end of the time frame. Although more than 60 individuals fit this description, a mere four were contacted in the first year of the panel when they were married, making conclusions about how contact rates changed after marriage altogether impossible.

What we can definitively conclude from this analysis is that fluctuating patterns of political mobilization by marital status is worth further study. If parties have adapted their mobilization strategies such that Democrats contact relatively more unmarried voters while Republicans mobilize relatively more married voters, it is not difficult to imagine why we would have a marriage gap in the vote.

There is some anecdotal evidence that marital status is, in fact, an aspect of the voter mobilization strategies of the major political parties and those of a range of other political organizations (such as interest groups). As more and more information about voters becomes available for commercial purchase, targeting based upon marital status is already feasible and will only become easier.

In fact, new interest groups recently have emerged that specifically center around marital status, such as Women's Voices, Women Vote (an organization dedicated to increasing political participation among all unmarried women), and the American Association for Single People (an organization dedicated to lobbying to advance the interests of unmarried persons).

THE FUTURE OF THE MARRIAGE GAP AND RELATED RESEARCH

If present trends continue, the unmarried portion of the American population will continue to grow, and there is little evidence to indicate any near-term migration of these voters away from the Democratic Party. The picture is somewhat different for married America, however. In the last several election cycles, married voters have looked slightly less like Republican base voters and more like swing voters. The 2006 congressional elections provided a case in point: Republican candidates won among married voters by only two points, according to the exit polls,[26] and Democracy Corps polls indicate that married women in particular were swing voters in 2006.

Whether married America returns to its Republican roots or retains its new status as a swing segment may depend in part on the assumptions and strategies of the major political parties. If the Democrats write off married America while Republicans seek to woo these voters back, then married America may begin once again to give large margins of their support to Republican candidates. However, if Democrats aggressively pursue persuadable married voters, they may be swing voters for some time to come.

More scholarly insight into the psychological effects of marriage on political attitudes would be a welcome addition to the current literature. Political scientists Laura Stoker and M. Kent Jennings demonstrate that patterns of political participation appear to be closely connected to changes in lifestyle, particularly marriage,[27] but a companion study on political attitudes themselves would be extremely informative. Scholars have observed the cross-sectional relationships between political attitudes and marital status (as I have documented above) and made assertions about why we observe these relationships, but no study has followed adults who have changed their marital status to test the merits of these arguments about political attitudes and voting behavior. The closest study has been the Stoker and Jennings study, which did utilize panel data to examine individuals whose marital status changed, but they used it to examine changes in participation, not attitudes; a companion study of attitudes would be especially informative. It would also be worth learning how political attitudes change when married adults become divorced, widowed, or separated. In the ANES panel studies discussed above, there were an insufficient number of respondents who had undergone such a transition, even pooling across observations in both panels.

As rates of cohabitation increase, it also may be relevant to study whether cohabitating citizens' political attitudes and behaviors more closely resemble those of married or unmarried adults. Although much is known about the significance and effects of cohabitation from a sociological perspective, little is known about how cohabitation affects political orientations. Panel studies that track couples before and during (and, potentially after) cohabitation would shed light on how this phenomenon impacts political attitudes and beliefs.

Notes

[1] I will offer evidence for this assertion using data from the American National Election Studies later in this chapter.

[2] Dennis Cauchon, "Marriage Gap Could Sway Elections," *USA Today* (September 27, 2006): 1A.

[3] Anna Greenberg, "The Marriage Gap: How to Make Family Values and Moral Renewal Democratic Issues," *Blueprint Magazine*, http://www.ndol.org/ndol_ci.cfm?kaid=114&subid=144&contentid=3559 (2001); Anna Greenberg and Jennifer Berktold, "Is the Marriage Gap More Important Than the Gender Gap? The Effect of Family Structure on Voting," in *Gender Gap: Voting and the Sexes*, ed. Lois Duke-Whitaker (Urbana: University of Illinois Press, 2007); Jonathan Rauch, "The Widening Marriage Gap: America's New Class Divide," *National Journal* (May 23, 2001).

[4] Torbin Iversen and Frances Rosenbluth, "The Political Economy of Gender: Explaining Cross-National Variation in the Gender Division of Labor and the Gender Voting Gap," *American Journal of Political Science* 50 (2006): 1–19; Herbert F. Weisberg, "The Demographics of a New Voting Gap: Marital Differences in American Voting," *Public Opinion Quarterly* 51 (1987): 335–343.

[5] Eric Plutzer and Michael McBurnett, "Family Life and American Politics: The 'Marriage Gap' Reconsidered," *Public Opinion Quarterly* 55 (1991): 113–127; Jim Tinnick, "The Marriage Gap: Fact or Fiction?" *Perspectives* 6 (2003), http://aabss.org/journal2003/Tinnick.htm.

[6] "Marriage Gap Bigger than Gender Gap, with Married People More Supportive than Singles Are to Bush and Republicans, Annenberg Data Show," *National Annenberg Election Survey* (Washington, DC: Annenberg Public Policy Center, 2004); Susan Page, "Married? Single? Status Affects How Women Vote," *USA Today* (August 25, 2004): A1; Ruth Rosen, "Women Really

on Their Own," Longview Institute, http://www.longviewinstitute.org/research/rosen/
womenontheirown (2001); John Zogby, "The Marriage Gap and 2004 Presidential Politics,"
St. Louis Business Journal (February 27, 2004).

[7]Average life expectancy in 1900 was 47.3 years, compared to 77.5 years in 2003. See U.S. Department of Health and Human Services, Centers for Disease Control and Prevention, National Center for Health Statistics, *Health, United States, 2005, with Chartbook on Trends in the Health of Americans*, http://www.cdc.gov/nchs/data/hus/hus05.pdf#027 (2006).

[8]U.S. Census Bureau, "America's Families and Living Arrangements: 2003," http://www.census.gov/prod/2004pubs/p20-553.pdf (2004).

[9]Ibid.

[10]*Statistical Abstract of the United States 2006* (Washington, DC: U.S. Bureau of the Census, 2006).

[11]Ibid.

[12]Karen Oppenheim Mason and Yu-Hsia Lu, "Attitudes toward Women's Familial Roles: Changes in the United States, 1977-1985," *Gender and Society* 2 (1988): 39–57; Paul A. Nokenezny, Robert D. Shull, and Joseph Lee Rodgers, "The Effect of No-Fault Divorce Law on the Divorce Rate across the 50 States and Its Relation to Income, Education, and Religiosity," *Journal of Marriage and the Family* 57 (1995): 477–488.

[13]*Statistical Abstract of the United States 2006* (2006); see also Jerry A. Jacobs, "Gender Inequality and Higher Education," *Annual Review of Sociology* 22 (1996): 153–185.

[14]Mason and Lu (1988).

[15]*Statistical Abstract of the United States 2006* (2006).

[16]Some research suggests that although college-educated women are marrying later, they are more likely to marry eventually than are their counterparts without college degrees; see Joshua A. Goldstein and Catherine Kenney, "Marriage Delayed or Marriage Forgone? New Cohort Forecasts of First Marriage for U.S. Women," *American Sociological Review* 66 (2001): 504–519.

[17]See, for example, Claudia Goldin and Lawrence F. Katz, "The Power of the Pill: Oral Contraceptives and Women's Career and Marriage Decisions," *Journal of Political Economy* 110 (2002): 730–770.

[18]These themes are discussed in the popular press with great regularity, and there have been a number of good academic treatments as well. See Andrea Press and Terry Strathman, "Work, Family, and Social Class in Television Images of Women: Prime-Time Television and the Construction of Postfeminism," *Women and Language* 16 (1993): 7–15. Some of this literature suggests that television shows glorifying single life, sex, and new norms regarding marriage and family are less the result of the sexual revolution and the advent of contraceptives, but instead are related to the fragmentation of the media market. See, for example, Jane Arthurs, "*Sex and the City* and Consumer Culture: Remediating Post-Feminist Drama," *Feminist Media Studies* 3 (2003): 83–98.

[19]*Current Population Survey, 2004* (Washington, DC: U.S. Bureau of the Census, 2004).

[20]See Greenberg and Berktold (2007); Paul William Kingston and Steven E. Finkel, "Is There a Marriage Gap in Politics?" *Journal of Marriage and the Family* 49 (1987): 57–64.

[21]*Current Population Survey, 2004* (2004).

[22]Greenberg and Berktold (2007); see also Anna Greenberg, "Women on Their Own and the Presidential Election: A Survey of 12 States," http://www.gqrr.com/index.php?ID=1237 (2004); Amy Gershkoff, "Reaching Unmarried Women in 2006," http://www.gqrr.com/index.php?ID=1794 (2006).

[23]Greenberg and Berktold (2007).

[24]Edison Media Research and Mitofsky International. 2004. *Election 2004 Exit Polls.*

[25]Greenberg and Berktold (2007); Plutzer and McBurnett (1991); Tinnick (2003).

[26]Greenberg (2001); Greenberg and Berktold (2007).

[27]Laura Stoker and M. Kent Jennings, "Life-Cycle Transitions and Political Participation: The Case of Marriage," *American Political Science Review* 89 (1995): 421–433.

4

THE WORSHIP ATTENDANCE GAP

❧

LAURA R. OLSON
JOHN C. GREEN

As the 2004 presidential election approached, journalists paid a great deal of attention to what appeared to be a new political phenomenon: the "religion" or "God" gap. Americans who were most involved in religious life seemed especially likely to support Republican candidates at the polls and hold more conservative views, while those who were less involved in organized religion were more likely to vote Democratic and hold liberal views. As a typical news story put it, "Want to know how Americans will vote next Election Day? Watch what they do the weekend before. If they attend religious services regularly, they probably will vote Republican by a 2–1 margin. If they never go [to services], they likely will vote Democratic by a 2–1 margin."[1]

Public opinion polls provided ample evidence of the existence of this voting gap in the results of the 2004 election, and the press ran with the story. For example, a Pew Research Center poll found that the frequency of worship attendance was an especially powerful predictor of party preference on the eve of Election Day 2004.[2] Journalists quickly renamed this worship attendance gap the "religion gap" and eventually the "God gap." Of course, it does not take a great imagination to leap from talking about the political importance of *worship attendance*, which is, after all, one of the most important public expressions of faith, to thinking instead about the broader political significance of *belief in God*, which is the central feature of faith for most Americans.[3]

The God gap terminology attracted the most media attention because it suggested that the Republicans had become the party of America's "believers" and the Democrats the party of its "nonbelievers." Here, too, there was some evidence suggesting that Americans view the Republican Party as more "friendly to religion," but to think that the GOP is "God's party" and the Democratic Party is comprised only of nonreligious Americans is a vast overstatement.[4] Nonetheless, these news stories did correctly recognize the significance of religion in the 2004 presidential campaign.[5]

Through much of the twentieth century, religion's influence on elections operated largely through voters' religious affiliation, with the specific teachings of different religious traditions and denominations generating divergent voting patterns.[6] In the 1930s and 1940s, for instance, Catholics were loyal Democrats and mainline Protestants voted Republican. The media's God gap story, however, seemed to suggest something quite novel. Differences *within* religious communities were now apparently more politically significant than differences *among* religious traditions.[7] It did not matter whether one identified as a Catholic, Baptist, Methodist, Mormon, or something else, but rather how *committed* one was to religious life in general. Specifically, individuals who said they frequently attend worship services—across the various families of Christianity—were demonstrably more conservative in their politics than less frequent worshipers.

It is hardly surprisingly that such stark imagery prompted extensive criticism. Some critics pointed out that both major political parties do have religious constituencies.[8] For example, some of the most religious people in the United States, African-American Protestants, are heavily Democratic.[9] Moreover, many denominations actively teach moderate-to-liberal positions on a whole range of issues, which might easily produce support for the Democratic Party.[10] Critics also took aim at the God gap *language*, arguing that if a large majority of Americans claim to believe in God,[11] then belief in God by itself must not create political differences.[12]

Although these criticisms do carry a certain amount of weight, it is worthwhile to analyze the reality behind today's worship attendance gap. For one thing, such a voter gap is quite real,[13] and it is a relatively *new* feature of the contemporary political scene—indeed, one that may mark off a new era in American politics. Also, since worship attendance is measured in most public opinion polls, it is a straightforward exercise to measure this phenomenon empirically and analyze its meaning. And like other voting gaps (especially the generation gap and the gender gap), the worship attendance gap helps us to understand how aspects of everyday life relate to political behavior. Attending religious services and otherwise being involved in organized religious life is an important aspect of many Americans' lives. In fact, the United States stands out among developed nations for the depth of its citizenry's religious commitment.[14] How does this aspect of ordinary life affect the way people act in the political realm?

THE SOCIOLOGICAL ROOTS OF THE WORSHIP ATTENDANCE GAP

In 1988, sociologist Robert Wuthnow published an important book in which he argued that American religion had been transformed in important ways over the course of the twentieth century.[15] For many decades, Americans had thought of religious divisions primarily along the lines of a threefold "Protestant-Catholic-Jewish" framework.[16] What mattered most under this rubric was one's membership in one of these broad religious traditions and their major denominations. However, by the end of World War II extensive changes had occurred in American society that led two separate strains to emerge *within* major religious traditions: theological conservatives, who did not appreciate changes in American society or deviations from traditional moral codes, and theological liberals or progressives, who were committed to embracing social change and less concerned with traditional morality. Wuthnow shows that these new divisions were present within all of the major American religious traditions as well as in most large denominations. These divisions eventually became politically relevant, so that conservative Catholics found that they had more in common politically with conservative Baptists than they did with liberal Catholics—and vice versa.

A recent example of these new divisions is evident in the Episcopal Church. The Episcopal Church has deep roots in American history: ten U.S. presidents (including George Washington and Franklin D. Roosevelt) have been Episcopalians, as have a disproportionate number of U.S. Senators, members of the House of Representatives, governors, and Supreme Court justices. In recent decades, conservatives and liberals within the Episcopal Church have been deeply divided over many matters, and the deepest discord surrounds the issue of homosexuality. In 2003, the Episcopal Church named an openly gay man, Rev. Canon V. Gene Robinson, as its Bishop of New Hampshire. Since then, scores of Episcopal congregations across the United States have cut their ties with the national church and instead affiliated themselves with African and South American branches of the Worldwide Anglican Communion. In addition, the Episcopal Church came into conflict with other elements of the Anglican Communion (which is rooted in the Church of England). Some observers even argue that the Episcopal Church itself eventually will break in two.[17]

As Wuthnow argued, conservative Episcopalians who oppose gay rights would today have more in common, especially when it comes to politics, with conservatives from other religious traditions (for example, conservative Catholics) than they would with liberal Episcopalians who support gay rights. Across the board it has become more difficult to make political generalizations based on religious affiliation alone than it was in the mid-twentieth century. If religious "belonging" (affiliation) is no longer a reliable predictor of political attitudes and behaviors, then perhaps some other measure of "religion," such as religious beliefs or religious behavior, might be more politically relevant.[18]

Conservative religiosity has become more prominent in the United States in recent times. Since the 1970s, conservative congregations have been growing much more rapidly and visibly in the United States than have liberal congregations, including the much discussed "mega-churches" that we see springing up across the country. Indeed, conservative congregations have been shown to do an especially good job of attracting and retaining members for a generation or more.[19] There is also some evidence that religious conservatives tend to participate more frequently in various aspects of traditional religious life than do religious liberals.[20] Meaningful expressions of religious commitment include not only frequent attendance at worship services, but also frequent prayer, frequent reading of scripture, and regular consumption of religious media. Participating in organized religious life seems to offer many Americans an experience that differs substantially from the workaday world. Unlike the "me first," "dog-eat-dog" attitude endemic to American culture, organized religion openly encourages people to care for one another both spiritually and materially.[21] Conservative congregations also teach traditional morality, offering a clear alternative to the "sinfulness" of popular culture. All of these factors tend to reinforce one another: in conservative congregations, "strictness increases commitment, raises levels of participation, and enables [congregations] to offer more benefits to [both] current and potential members."[22]

The emphasis of conservative congregations on "traditional values" has translated easily into conservative views on some political issues, especially those involving family arrangements and sexuality. Such issues have become increasingly relevant in American politics overall because advocacy for liberal social values has become more common in recent times, most recently in the form of argument for same-sex marriage and civil unions.[23] Indeed, on the whole, Americans who support gay rights and abortion rights are less religious overall than Americans who oppose gay rights and abortion rights.[24]

THE POLITICAL ROOTS OF THE WORSHIP ATTENDANCE GAP

In the past decade, the voting gap between people who participate frequently in organized religious life and those who do not has become one of the more significant points of division in American politics. President George W. Bush was indebted to millions of conservative evangelical Protestant and Catholic voters following his reelection in November 2004.[25] The Bush–Cheney campaign worked diligently to mobilize these traditionalist Christians, and they turned out to vote for Bush in large numbers.[26] Karl Rove, President Bush's chief campaign advisor, knew that attempting to mobilize conservative people of faith in their congregations would be a fruitful electoral strategy because such individuals are both religiously and *politically* conservative.

Especially over the past three decades, religious conservatism and political conservatism have gone hand-in-glove. This close connection between religious and political conservatism traces its history to the emergence of a social movement known as the religious Right (or alternatively, the Christian right). Religious Right activists and organizations have a goal of restoring what they see as "traditional moral values" to public policy. The movement's opposition to abortion and gay rights is well known and rooted in a worldview that rejects nontraditional interpretations of gender roles, family structure, and sexual morality.

The religious Right first emerged in the late 1970s. Its best-known leader in this era was Rev. Jerry Falwell, a Baptist minister and religious broadcaster from Lynchburg, Virginia, who founded what quickly became a high-profile political organization, the Moral Majority. Along with several smaller interest groups, the Moral Majority mobilized millions to vote for Ronald Reagan in 1980 and 1984. Since the early 1980s, the religious Right has been transformed at least twice. First, Rev. Pat Robertson replaced Falwell as the movement's most visible spokesperson when he founded his own interest group, the Christian Coalition. The Christian Coalition became one of the most powerful lobbies in Washington in the 1990s. It also solidified conservative religious people's commitment to the Republican Party and its candidates, in large part because of the "voting guides" it published and distributed in churches across the United States. The influence of the Christian Coalition was in decline by 2000, but the movement as a whole was revived by the debate over same-sex marriage. In this context, the interest group Focus on the Family, its leader Dr. James Dobson, and a network of related organizations gained prominence. By 2004, the religious Right's strength came from a combination of national, state, and local organizations, as well as its widespread influence within Republican Party organizations.[27]

THE EMERGENCE OF THE WORSHIP ATTENDANCE GAP

Worship attendance is a common form of religious behavior in the United States. Typically at least 40 percent of Americans tell pollsters that they attend worship services once a week or more often. Although there is some question about the accuracy of these reports,[28] the worship attendance pattern has been quite consistent for decades.[29]

Figure 4.1 charts the emergence of the worship attendance gap from 1952 to 2004 using data from the American National Election Studies (ANES). The figure illustrates the *overall* level of support for the Democratic and Republican presidential candidates and the level of support for each candidate among survey respondents who *attend worship services* "regularly" (as the survey question was worded from 1952 through 1968) or "every week" (as the question has been worded since 1972). The figure clearly illustrates the fact that there was no sustained worship attendance gap in presidential voting behavior until 1992. Richard Nixon did better among frequent attendees in 1972, and Ronald Reagan enjoyed a similar advantage among frequent attendees in 1980, but the worship attendance gap really does not emerge as a clear feature of American presidential voting behavior until 1992 and thereafter.

FIGURE 4.1   WORSHIP ATTENDANCE AND PRESIDENTIAL VOTING, 1952–2004

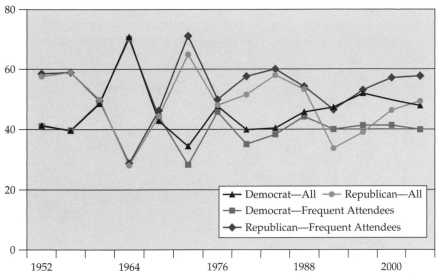

Source: Data from the 1952–2004 American National Election Studies.

To some extent, this finding contradicts conventional wisdom and a good bit of scholarly research indicating that Reagan's presidency initiated the political cleavage between America's most religious voters and their more secular counterparts.[30] The roots of the worship attendance gap (and certainly those of the religious Right movement that helped to spawn it) may well lie in Reagan's 1980 presidential candidacy, but it apparently took a dozen years for actual statistical evidence of this gap to appear. It is ironic that George H. W. Bush—who, unlike his son, was not noted for public displays of religiosity—was one of the first to benefit from a double-digit advantage (12.8 percentage points) among frequent worship attendees, as compared with the public at large.

It is especially useful to consider the worship attendance gap in the context of the most committed evangelical Protestant and Catholic voters. There have been particularly noteworthy changes in the voting behavior of these two religious traditions in recent decades. Evangelicals have undergone a thorough political realignment since the 1980s, becoming one of the most loyal of the Republican Party's constituencies.[31] Meanwhile, Catholics have been transformed from a stalwart contingent of the Democrats' New Deal Coalition to a true swing constituency.[32]

Figure 4.2 illustrates the gaps between the voting behavior of the electorate at large and that of evangelical Protestant and Catholic frequent attendees using 1980–2004 ANES data. Here the worship attendance gap is particularly striking, revealing that the Republican Party indeed has done a remarkably effective job of appealing to the most committed evangelical and Catholic

FIGURE 4.2   REPUBLICAN PRESIDENTIAL VOTING AMONG EVANGELICAL
PROTESTANT AND CATHOLIC FREQUENT ATTENDEES, 1980–2004

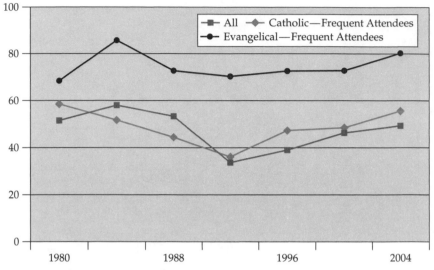

Source: Data from the 1952–2004 American National Election Studies.

voters in the American electorate.[33] The closest the "frequently attending evangelical vote" has been to the overall sample vote in 24 years is 16 percentage points—and that was in 1980. The voting gap between frequently attending Catholics and the overall sample has been smaller, but no less persistent. Frequently attending Catholics have favored the Republican candidate in every election since 1980—and they favored George W. Bush over fellow Catholic John Kerry by 6.3 percentage points more than did the overall sample in 2004. No one would have predicted such a result three decades ago, when Catholics remained stalwartly Democratic regardless of their specific religious beliefs or behaviors.

THE WORSHIP ATTENDANCE GAP IN 2004

To what extent was the worship attendance gap a decisive factor in the religion-infused 2004 presidential election? According to the exit poll data reported in Table 4.1, 16.2 percent of voters in 2004 claimed to attend worship services more than once a week and another 26.6 percent said they worshiped once a week. Thus, "weekly attendees" comprised 42.8 percent of the 2004 electorate. On the opposite end of the scale, 15.0 percent of 2004 voters claimed never to attend worship services, while 28.3 percent said they attended only a few times a year. These figures total 43.3 percent, comprising almost the same proportion of the electorate as the weekly attendees. The remaining

TABLE 4.1   WORSHIP ATTENDANCE AND PRESIDENTIAL VOTE, 2004

	(FREQUENCY)	PERCENT VOTING FOR BUSH	PERCENT VOTING FOR KERRY
More than once a week	(16.2)	64.7	35.3
Once a week	(26.6)	58.9	41.1
A few times a month	(13.9)	50.7	49.3
A few times a year	(28.3)	45.2	54.8
Never	(15.0)	36.6	63.4
All	(100.0)	51.5	48.5

Source: Data from the 2004 National Election Pool Data.

"middle" category (those who report worshiping a few times a month) accounted for the remaining 13.9 percent of the electorate.

Thus, worship attendance did divide voters fairly evenly in 2004. And each level of attendance is clearly associated with the vote for George W. Bush and John F. Kerry. The pattern is striking and nearly symmetrical. Just under two-thirds (64.7 percent) of voters (regardless of their specific religious affiliation) who attended worship services more than once a week backed Bush, compared to a bit more than one-third (35.3 percent) who supported Kerry. Meanwhile, among voters who never worship, just over a third voted for Bush (36.6 percent) and nearly two-thirds (63.4 percent) voted for Kerry. In fact, the vote for Bush declined steadily as the frequency of reported worship attendance decreased—and the Kerry vote increased in exactly the opposite fashion. Notice as well how close the contest was among voters in the middle attendance category (those who worship several times a month). Here Bush bested Kerry by less than one percent!

These data reveal an extensive worship attendance gap in the two-party presidential vote. The difference between the Bush vote among the most and least frequent worship attendees was 28 percentage points. Moreover, fully half of *all* of Bush's ballots were cast by weekly worship attendees, whereas less-than-weekly attendees cast some two-thirds of all Kerry's votes. These results are valuable because we know for certain that exit poll respondents actually came to the polls, a fact that is more difficult to assure with other survey data (including ANES).

As impressive as these figures are, it is important not to overstate their significance. President Bush could not have been reelected without the support he received from less-frequent worshipers. Likewise, the election would not have been nearly as close if Kerry had not received a substantial number of votes from frequent worship attendees, suggesting that there still might be some semblance of a "religious left" in the United States.[34] Nevertheless, these results reveal clear evidence of the empirical reality of the worship attendance gap.

These results would imply that the worship attendance gap bears a strong association to political attitudes, with weekly worship attendees holding more conservative views and less-than-weekly attendees espousing more liberal attitudes. There was a good bit of truth behind this assumption in 2004, but the truth of the matter must be interpreted with considerable nuance. Table 4.2 reveals that frequency of worship attendance was closely associated with self-reported ideology in 2004. Nearly half (45.2 percent) of the weekly attendees said they were conservative, compared to just a quarter (24.9 percent) of the less-than-weekly attendees. However, another two-fifths (41.2 percent) of the weekly attendees claimed the "moderate" label. Here the less-than-weekly attendees were more numerous, with just about one-half (49.1 percent) reporting moderate political views. In contrast, only about one-seventh (13.6 percent) of all weekly attendees were liberal, a proportion only half the size of the liberal contingent among less-than-weekly attendees (25.9 percent). These patterns, of course, are skewed a bit by that fact that only one-fifth of the electorate self-identified as liberal in 2004. Evidently the "L" word remains a dirty word in American politics.

A similar pattern holds for the self-reported issue priorities of 2004 voters. Just over a third (34.4 percent) of the weekly attendees said that "moral values" were the most important motivation for their vote—more than twice the number of "moral values" voters among less-frequent attendees (15.7 percent). However, almost as many weekly attendees chose an economic issue (such as the economy, jobs, or health insurance), and others chose a foreign policy issue (such as terrorism or the war in Iraq). Note, however, that economic

TABLE 4.2   WORSHIP ATTENDANCE AND POLITICAL ATTITUDES, 2004

IDEOLOGY	CONSERVATIVE	MODERATE	LIBERAL
Regular attendees	45.2%	41.2%	13.6%
Less-frequent attendees	24.9%	49.1%	25.9%
All	33.6%	45.7%	20.7%

POLICY PRIORITIES	MORAL ISSUES	ECONOMIC POLICY	FOREIGN POLICY
Regular attendees	34.4%	34.3%	31.3%
Less-frequent attendees	15.7%	44.3%	40.0%
All	23.7%	40.0%	36.3%

PARTISANSHIP	REPUBLICAN	INDEPENDENT	DEMOCRAT
Regular attendees	46.5%	21.3%	32.2%
Less-frequent attendees	30.8%	28.7%	40.5%
All	37.5%	25.6%	36.9%

Source: Data from the 2004 National Election Pool Data.

issues (44.3 percent) and foreign policy (40.0 percent) were markedly more common priorities of the less-than-weekly attendees.

The clearest difference in Table 4.2 emerges around partisanship. Nearly half (46.5 percent) of the weekly attendees considered themselves Republicans, compared to less than a third (30.8 percent) of the less-than-weekly attendees. On the other hand, just about a third (32.2 percent) of the weekly attendees were Democrats, compared to two-fifths (40.5 percent) of the less-regular attendees.

WILL THE WORSHIP ATTENDANCE GAP PERSIST IN THE FUTURE?

Our evidence of the worship attendance gap begs several important questions. Does it have an independent impact on politics, or is it simply a by-product of other factors that bear upon people's voting preferences? Even if religious commitment does have an independent effect on vote choice, what is the relationship between the worship attendance gap and other demographic and political factors? Does the worship attendance gap counter or reinforce the political effects of other factors such as gender or social class?[35] The most important question, however, revolves around what the worship attendance gap tells us about the political role of religion. On this score, three potential answers come to mind.

First, the worship attendance gap actually may reflect some continuing political significance of religious affiliation. After all, most people attend worship in a particular congregation, which probably belongs to a denomination, and in turn, a larger religious tradition. Such religious communities and institutions have long been the most important means of linking religion to politics.[36] The worship attendance gap therefore may be capturing some of the effects of religious affiliation. It may be, for instance, that weekly attendees are concentrated in certain religious communities and not in others, or it might be that less-frequent attendees are not particularly influenced by the distinctive values of religious communities. The role of religious affiliation may help explain both the power and the limitations of the worship attendance gap insofar as some weekly attendees may belong to congregations that encourage moderate or liberal political values.

Second, the worship attendance gap may reflect the political significance of religious belief. It may be, for instance, that weekly worship attendees are more likely to hold certain sorts of religious beliefs, while less-than-weekly attendees are more likely to hold contrary beliefs.[37] Here, too, the impact of religious beliefs may help explain why the religion gap is important but not comprehensive in its effects: some weekly attendees may espouse religious beliefs that foster liberal or moderate political views.

Third, the worship attendance gap may reflect the political significance of religious commitment quite apart from the impact of religious affiliation or belief. High levels of religious commitment, of which weekly worship attendance is just one component, may foster particular connections between religion and politics by exposing individuals to special kinds of information. Such information might be a by-product of religious life, such as sermon messages or the content of conversations with fellow attendees.[38] Or it might be the result of deliberate efforts to motivate political action, such as official pronouncements on issues or voter guides distributed in congregations.[39] If so, weekly worship attendees are more likely to be exposed to this special information than are less-than-weekly attendees. And the political significance of religious commitment may also help explain why the impact of the worship attendance gap is strong but not uniform: weekly attendees may receive different kinds of politically relevant information.

It is also worth noting that despite the gains made by the Democratic Party in the midterm elections of 2006, the worship attendance gap persisted.[40] If the appearance of the worship attendance gap does in fact mark the beginning of a new political era with a new kind of connection between religion and politics, then it is critical to understand its religious underpinnings. After all, religion's political consequences are significant—and are likely to remain so at least in the near future. We fully expect the worship attendance gap to continue to exert a powerful effect on voting behavior in 2008 and beyond.

NOTES

[1]Steven Thomma, "Americans' Religious Practices Serve as Gauge of Political Choice," *The Philadelphia Inquirer* (December 1, 2003): A2.

[2]Pew Research Center for the People and the Press, "2004 Political Landscape: Evenly Divided and Increasingly Polarized," http://people-press.org/reports/display.php3?ReportID=196 (2003).

[3]Robert Booth Fowler, Allen D. Hertzke, Laura R. Olson, and Kevin R. den Dulk, *Religion and Politics in America: Faith, Culture, and Strategic Choices*, 3rd ed. (Boulder, CO: Westview, 2004).

[4]Pew Forum on Religion and Public Life, "Religion and the 2006 Elections," http://pewforum.org/docs/index.php?DocID=174 (2006).

[5]See David E. Campbell, ed., *A Matter of Faith: Religion in the 2004 Presidential Election* (Washington, DC: Brookings Institution, 2007) and John C. Green, *The Faith Factor: How Religion Influences American Elections* (Westport, CT: Praeger, 2007).

[6]Will Herberg, *Protestant-Catholic-Jew: An Essay in American Religious Sociology* (Garden City, NY: Doubleday, 1955); Robert Wuthnow, *The Restructuring of American Religion: Society and Faith since World War II* (Princeton, NJ: Princeton University Press, 1988).

[7]The point was novel to many observers, but had already been documented by a range of scholars. See John C. Green, James L. Guth, Corwin E. Smidt, and Lyman A. Kellstedt, *Religion and the Culture Wars: Dispatches from the Front* (Lanham, MD: Rowman and Littlefield, 1996); James Davison Hunter, *Culture Wars: The Struggle to Define America* (New York: Basic Books, 1991); Andrew Kohut, John C. Green, Scott Keeter, and Robert C. Toth, *The Diminishing Divide: Religion's Changing Role in American Politics* (Washington, DC: Brookings Institution, 2000); Geoffrey Layman, *The Great Divide: Religious and Cultural Conflict in American Party Politics* (New York: Columbia University Press, 2001); David C. Leege and Lyman A. Kellstedt, eds., *Rediscovering the Religious Factor in American Politics* (Armonk, NY: M. E. Sharpe, 1993); David C. Leege, Kenneth D. Wald, Brian S. Krueger, and Paul D. Mueller, *The Politics of Cultural Differences* (Princeton, NJ: Princeton University Press, 2002); Wuthnow (1988).

[8]Terry Eastland, "The God Gap," *The Weekly Standard*, www.theweeklystandard.com/Content/Public/Articles/000/000/004/549seugc.asp (September 1, 2004); Gerald L. Zelizer, "'The God Gap': A Political Myth," *USA Today*, www.usatoday.com/news/opinion/editorials/2004-07-13-zelizer_x.htm (July 13, 2004).

[9]Fredrick C. Harris, *Something Within: Religion in African-American Political Activism* (New York: Oxford University Press, 1999).

[10]Such religious traditions include Judaism: L. Sandy Maisel and Ira N. Forman, eds., *Jews in American Politics: Essays* (Lanham, MD: Rowman and Littlefield, 2003); mainline Protestantism: Jeff Manza and Clem Brooks, "The Changing Political Fortunes of Mainline Protestants," in *The Quiet Hand of God: Faith-Based Activism and the Public Role of Mainline Protestantism*, eds. Robert Wuthnow and John H. Evans (Berkeley: University of California Press, 2002); and to a more limited extent, Catholicism: Clarke E. Cochran and David Carroll Cochran, *Catholics, Politics, and Public Policy: Beyond Left and Right* (Maryknoll, NY: Orbis, 2003).

[11]As they do: Fowler et al. (2004) report that 95 percent of Americans believe in God or a "universal spirit" (p. 27).

[12]Amy Sullivan, "Left Church," *The American Prospect*, www.prospect.org/web/page .ww?section=root&name=ViewPrint&articleId=9893 (July 3, 2005).

[13]Morris P. Fiorina, *Culture War? The Myth of a Polarized America* (New York: Pearson Longman, 2005); John C. Green, "The American Religious Landscape and Political Attitudes: A Baseline for 2004," www.uakron.edu/bliss/research.php (2004); John C. Green and Mark Silk, "The New Religion Gap," *Religion in the News* 5 (2003): 3; John C. Green, Corwin E. Smidt, James L. Guth, and Lyman A. Kellstedt, "The American Religious Landscape and the 2004 Presidential Vote," www.uakron.edu/bliss/research.php (2004); Kohut et al. (2000); Layman (2001).

[14]Pippa Norris and Ronald Inglehart, *Sacred and Secular* (New York: Cambridge University Press, 2004).

[15]Wuthnow (1988).

[16]Herberg (1955).

[17]Laurie Goodstein and Neela Banerjee, "Anglican Plan Threatens Split on Gay Issues," *New York Times* (June 26, 2006): A1; Neela Banerjee, "Anglican Church Intercedes as an Episcopal Rift Widens," *New York Times* (May 5, 2007): A14.

[18]Leege and Kellstedt (1993) were the first to use this "three Bs" rubric to describe the major dimensions of American religious life: belonging, believing, and behaving. Also see Green, *The Faith Factor* for a fuller description of these categories.

[19]Dean M. Kelley, *Why Conservative Churches Are Growing: A Study in Sociology of Religion* (New York: Harper and Row, 1972); Laurence R. Iannaccone, "Why Strict Churches Are Strong," *American Journal of Sociology* 99 (1994): 1180–1211.

[20]See Green (2007): Chapter 3.

[21]See Robert Booth Fowler, *Unconventional Partners: Religion and Liberal Culture in the United States* (Grand Rapids, MI: Eerdmans, 1989).

[22]Iannaccone (1994): 1181.

[23]John C. Green, Mark J. Rozell, and Clyde Wilcox, eds., *The Values Campaign: The Christian Right in American Politics* (Washington, DC: Georgetown University Press, 2006); Ronald Inglehart, *Culture Shift in Advanced Industrial Society* (Princeton, NJ: Princeton University Press, 1990).

[24]Pew Research Center, "Trends in Political Values and Core Attitudes: 1987-2007," http://people-press.org/reports/display.php3?ReportID=312 (2007).

[25]Allen Cooperman and Thomas B. Edsall, "Evangelicals Say They Led Charge for the GOP," *Washington Post* (November 7, 2004): A1.

[26]Green et al. (2004); Pew Forum on Religion and Public Life, "How the Faithful Voted," http://pewforum.org/events/index.php?EventID=64 (2004).

[27]See John C. Green, Mark J. Rozell, and Clyde Wilcox, eds. *The Christian Right in American Politics: Marching to the Millennium* (Washington, DC: Georgetown University Press, 2003); Green, Rozell, and Wilcox (2006); Clyde Wilcox (1992), *God's Warriors: The Christian Right in Twentieth-Century America* (Baltimore, MD: Johns Hopkins University Press); Clyde Wilcox and Carin Larson, *Onward Christian Soldiers? The Religious Right in American Politics*, 3rd ed. (Boulder, CO: Westview, 2006).

[28]C. Kirk Hadaway, Penny Long Marler, and Mark Chaves, "What the Polls Don't Show: A Closer Look at U.S. Church Attendance," *American Sociological Review* 58 (1993): 741–752.

[29]Fowler et al. (2004).

[30]Leege et al. (2002); Layman (2001); Wilcox (1992); Wilcox and Larson (2006).

[31]Layman (2001).

[32]Kohut et al. (2000).

[33]See also Cooperman and Edsall (2004); Green et al. (2004); Kohut et al. (2000); Layman (2001); Pew Forum (2004); Pew Forum on Religion and Public Life, "Religion a Strength and Weakness for Both Parties," http://pewforum.org/docs/index.php?DocID=115 (2005).

[34]See Laura R. Olson, "Whither the Religious Left? Religiopolitical Progressivism in Twenty-First Century America," in *From Pews to Polling Places: Faith and Politics in the American Religious Mosaic*, ed. J. Matthew Wilson (Washington, DC: Georgetown University Press, 2007).

[35]See Chapter 1 of this volume for a discussion of the relative significance of the worship attendance gap vis-à-vis other voting gaps. The worship attendance gap is not likely to be just a by-product of other demographic voting gaps.

[36]Paul A. Djupe and Christopher P. Gilbert, *The Prophetic Pulpit: Clergy, Churches, and Communities in American Politics* (Lanham, MD: Rowman and Littlefield, 2003); Paul A. Djupe and Christopher P. Gilbert, "The Resourceful Believer: Generating Civic Skills in Church," *Journal of Politics* 68 (2006): 116–127; Paul A. Djupe and J. Tobin Grant, "Religious Institutions and Political Participation in America," *Journal for the Scientific Study of Religion* 40 (2001): 303–314; Kenneth D. Wald, Dennis E. Owen, and Samuel S. Hill, "Churches as Political Communities," *American Political Science Review* 82 (1988): 531–548; Kenneth D. Wald, Dennis E. Owen, and Samuel S. Hill, "Political Cohesion in Churches," *Journal of Politics* 52 (1990): 197–215.

[37]Kohut et al. (2000); Geoffrey C. Layman and John C. Green, "Wars and Rumors of Wars: The Contexts of Cultural Conflict in American Political Behavior," *British Journal of Political Science* 36 (2005): 61–89.

[38]Djupe and Gilbert (2003, 2006).

[39]James L. Guth, Lyman A. Kellstedt, John C. Green, and Corwin E. Smidt, "A Distant Thunder? Religious Mobilization in the 2000 Elections," in *Interest Group Politics*, 6th ed., eds. Allan J. Cigler and Burdett A. Loomis (Washington, DC: CQ Press, 2002).

[40]Pew Forum (2006).

5

THE CLASS GAP*

❖

HECTOR L. ORTIZ
JEFFREY M. STONECASH

Class-based political divisions would seem to be central to contemporary American politics. Inequalities in the distribution of income and wealth have grown steadily since the early 1970s, creating greater differences in opportunity for many individuals and challenging the long-standing American hope for equality of opportunity.[1] The two major political parties differ in their concern about class-related issues, making class-based political cleavages all the more likely. Today's conditions seem ripe for politicians—particularly Democrats—to focus on the notion of social class as a way to attract voters and build a larger electoral base. Voters with stagnant wages and those who have lost health care benefits and pensions would seem especially amenable to appeals based on class.

Yet, at the outset of the 2002 election campaign, Democratic Party leadership was engaged in a serious debate about whether Al Gore's close loss in 2000 was because he focused on populist issues too much.[2] Many high-profile Democrats, including Gore's own running mate, Joe Lieberman, argued that Gore could have won in 2000 if he had emphasized centrist rhetoric rather than populist appeals. From governors to pollsters, Democrats all blamed Gore's "the people versus the powerful" message for his defeat in key border states such as Missouri.

In preparation for the 2002 midterm election, the politically moderate and influential Democratic Leadership Council (DLC) resolved that continuing with Gore's populist rhetoric would further alienate "upscale voters" while failing to increase the Democratic vote among the working class. For 2002, the DLC agreed that instead of focusing on a "rich versus poor" message, the Democratic Party should emphasize the effects of the 2002 economic

*Previously published as J.M. Stonecash, "The Income Gap." *PS: Political Science and Politics* 39 (2006): 461–465. Reprinted with the permission of Cambridge University Press.

downturn on *all* income groups. This focus would be their key strategy in attempting to retain a Democratic majority in the U.S. Senate and gain extra seats in the U.S. House of Representatives.

While the DLC was seeking to back away from any hint of a class appeal, other observers argued that Gore's populism (which was in line with the appeals of many successful Democratic presidential candidates[3]) actually made the 2000 election a *closer* contest than it might have been. In fact, journalists and academics alike argued that Gore's populism was a revitalizing message for his campaign and the Democratic Party in general, and that instead of alienating voters it brought in larger numbers of "upscale voters" than Clinton had in 1996.[4]

This debate reflects a fundamental fact of American politics over the last several decades: there is profound disagreement about the extent and relevance of class divisions in American politics. Some argue that class divisions once were significant but gradually declined after the 1950s. Others argue that the trends are exactly the opposite. Candidates who are trying to decide what themes to emphasize in their campaigns would find it difficult to be certain whether appeals focused on class would be a mistake. Do class issues divide voters? Can a Democratic candidate use issues like the minimum wage, access to health care coverage, availability of grants to attend college, and access to pension systems to mobilize the less affluent? Can a Republican candidate use issues like tax cuts, repealing the estate tax, and business deregulation to appeal to the more affluent?

This chapter presents an overview of our current understanding of the role that class divisions play in American electoral politics. We begin by reviewing the development of research on class and note that many studies have reached the conclusion that class's relevance in American politics is declining. Next, we present evidence on the development of class divisions in American politics from the 1930s to the present, focusing on divisions by income. The analysis assesses how growing income inequality and divergence of party positions have affected class divisions—and their political significance—over time. As the two parties have become increasingly polarized, so too, class divisions have increased. Finally, we note that while there has been a general increase in class divisions over time, short-term factors and other trends affect the extent of division in any given election cycle. We address two issues that are affecting the current extent of class divisions: the war in Iraq and the new significance of socio-moral issues in American politics. Short-term issues such as the war in Iraq affect the extent of divisions, but so do longer-term issues like the ongoing culture war over "family values." The latter is particularly important because often it is argued that issues such as abortion and gay rights have motivated less-educated Americans to vote more Republican, resulting in a suppression of the political relevance of class divisions.

THE DEVELOPMENT OF CLASS ANALYSES

Throughout the 1980s and 1990s, scholars' dominant conclusion about class and politics was that class divisions were of declining relevance in American elections. While it was generally agreed that class divisions had been politically relevant from the 1930s through the 1950s, by the 1970s evidence was emerging that they were no longer especially significant. The argument was that post-war America had experienced a widespread increase in affluence, lessening the relevance of economic concerns as a source of political division. Economic divisions increasingly were seen as having been displaced by disagreements over issues intertwined with race, culture, and values.

In the years following World War II there were reasons to presume that conflicts over economic issues had grown less relevant than they had been in prior decades. While there had been enormous inequality and little income growth during the 1930s, World War II spurred the American economy. In the 1950s and 1960s, incomes steadily increased and inequality declined. In addition, in the decades after World War II, it appeared that Republicans generally had come to accept the continued existence of New Deal safety-net programs. Fundamental conflicts over the increased size and scope of government in the post–New Deal era appeared to have been resolved.

These economic trends were accompanied by analyses arguing that material concerns had become less salient in people's lives. Sociologist Daniel Bell argued that the great political issues were settled, and ideological conflicts were over.[5] Political scientist Robert Inglehart presented evidence that humanity had entered a postindustrial era in which people were more concerned with the quality of life than material concerns.[6] Other scholars also noted this diminished focus on economic issues, arguing that American society was now being dominated by new sets of issues that were transforming politics. The issue of race had emerged as a major source of division between the parties,[7] displacing class divisions,[8] as had been the case in the South for decades.[9] Other observers saw the post-1960s era as one in which cultural values (crime, abortion, homosexuality, pornography, and free speech) and political conflicts over them became predominant, presumably because economic conflicts were of less consequence than values disputes.[10] The strongest statement about the decline of traditional class divisions was made by political scientists Everett Ladd and Charles Hadley:

> There has been an inversion of the old New Deal relationship of social class to the vote. In wide sectors of public policy, groups of high socioeconomic status are now more supportive of egalitarian (liberal) change than are the middle to lower socioeconomic cohorts (within white America); and as a result liberal (often, although not always, Democratic) candidates are finding higher measures of electoral sustenance at the top of the socioeconomic ladder than among the middle and lower rungs.[11]

In short, scholars reached the general conclusion that class-based political divisions in the United States were declining and perhaps soon to be irrelevant. Some measured class by using self-identified social class,[12] while others used socioeconomic status.[13] Regardless of the approach, the conclusion was that class divisions had declined,[14] especially in presidential elections.[15] This decline was seen by many as part of the general unraveling of electoral attachments to the major political parties and a growing irrelevance of historical sources of political divisions among Americans.[16]

The conclusion that class issues had been displaced acquired more acceptance as studies in the 1990s argued that socio-moral issues were becoming ever more politically salient.[17] The argument was that social conservatives—those who think there are clear and unbending moral values and accompanying behaviors that all people should follow—increasingly were troubled by social behaviors they were witnessing, including legal abortion, assertions of gay rights, sex and violence on television and in the movies, no-fault divorce, and out-of-wedlock births. In response, social conservatives decried the "decline" of American behavior and society and began pushing for legislative action to constrain behaviors that troubled them as much as possible. Much of the motivation for these efforts came from Americans with strong religious commitments. In opposition were secular and less religious Americans who stressed the right of individuals to live their own lives according to their own moral codes. Those studying the developing "culture wars" argued that American voters increasingly were divided by socio-moral issues rather than by class.[18] Most importantly, some scholars argued that the less affluent were most likely to be agitated by these issues.[19] As Republicans began to stress these issues more and more with each successive campaign, they were able to draw more and more support from lower-income voters, thereby compressing the extent of class divisions in American politics.[20] Any politician following these debates might think it unwise to discuss class issues in a campaign.

THE EVIDENCE ON CLASS DIVISIONS

While a scholarly consensus developed that class was fading as a politically salient issue, that conclusion does not stand up well to the evidence. For one thing, there are reasons to question the way in which many scholars measured class. Most analyses measured class by using self-identified class or socioeconomic status, but each of these measures has significant limitations.[21] Perhaps the most appropriate indicator of class is income.[22] Income is what provides resources for families and provides opportunity for children within families. The analysis that follows uses family income as a reflection of the class situation of individuals in American society.

The scholars who concluded that class was no longer politically relevant also tended to neglect how the extent of this division might vary across different social and political conditions. Class divisions do not just emerge; they are affected by context. Class divisions are likely to be limited when inequality is declining and when the major political parties do not differ much on class-related public policy issues. Divisions are likely to be greater when inequality is growing and when the parties differ about how to ameliorate poverty. The United States has experienced considerable variation in both inequality and party differences over time, which should create corresponding differences in class divisions.

Briefly, during the 1930s and 1940s inequality and party differences were relatively large. From the 1950s through the 1970s, both inequality and party divisions were declining. Since the 1970s, however, both inequality and party differences about public policy have increased.[23] These long-term changes should have produced corresponding changes in class divisions—and their relative political consequence.[24]

Inequality declined from the 1940s through the 1960s, but beginning in the early 1970s inequality in the distribution of wealth[25] and income[26] began to increase. Less affluent Americans were experiencing virtually no increase in family income, even though more women were in the labor force (and therefore contributing to family income),[27] and despite the statistical fact that all Americans were working longer hours.[28] During the 1980s and 1990s, those occupying the bottom two income quintiles were experiencing no gains, while those with higher incomes were experiencing significant gains.[29]

The resulting pattern of inequality in the distribution of income (measured with the Gini index)[30] for the last century is shown in Figure 5.1. From

FIGURE 5.1   INEQUALITY IN THE DISTRIBUTION OF INCOME,
(THE GINI INDEX), 1913 TO 2004

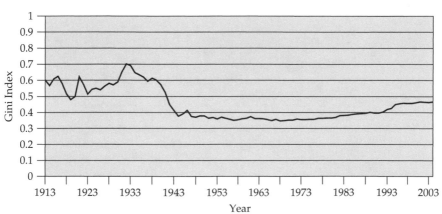

Sources: Robert D. Plotnick, Eugene Smolensky, Eirik Evenjouse, and Siobhan Reilly, "The Twentieth Century Record of Inequality and Poverty in the United States," Institute for Research on Poverty, Discussion Paper no. 1166–98, July, 1998: http://www.irp.wisc.edu/publications/dps/pdfs/dp116698.pdf; and, U.S. Census Bureau: http://www.census.gov/hhes/www/income/histinc/ineqtoc.html.

1913 until the early 1940s, the Gini index was relatively high, meaning that income inequality was high, with the highest levels of inequality appearing during the Great Depression. During the 1940s, inequality declined and remained at a relatively low level for roughly three decades. In the 1970s, however, it gradually began to creep up again, and has increased further almost every year since then. If the extent of income inequality affects class divisions, it should have been politically significant in the 1930s but then declined. Inequality is again clearly on the rise. There are regular debates in Congress about what sorts of programs might help specific income groups, which programs should be cut or increased, who will be hurt, and whether tax cuts should be enacted to benefit particular income groups.[31]

As income inequality has increased, the parties also have diverged in their policy concerns.[32] Republican and Democratic congressional candidates differ ideologically, of course, but their largest differences revolve around economic issues such as job training, housing assistance, and taxes.[33] The voting records of the two parties on such matters are becoming even more polarized.[34] In the House of Representatives, Democrats have become more liberal on economic issues over the last three decades as Republicans have become more conservative.

The specific differences between the two parties' positions on economic issues may be measured with precision using the DW-Nominate scores developed by political scientists Keith Poole and Howard Rosenthal.[35] Differences between the two parties regarding economic issues follow a pattern very similar to that of actual income inequality.[36] As Figure 5.2 indicates, party

FIGURE 5.2 AVERAGE PARTY DW-NOMINATE SCORES,
HOUSE OF REPRESENTATIVES, 1900–2002

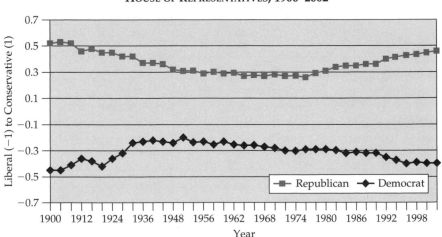

Source: Data from Keith Poole, taken from: http://voteview.com/dwnl.htm.

FIGURE 5.3   VOTER AWARENESS OF PARTY DIFFERENCES, 1952–2004

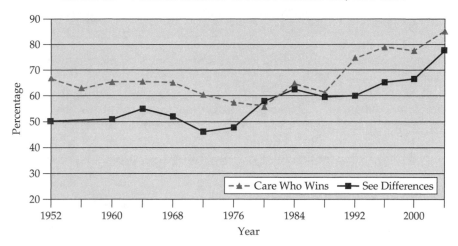

Source: NES Cumulative File, 1948–2004.

differences were relatively large during the first half of the twentieth century and then gradually declined from the 1940s through most of the 1970s. Then the differences began to increase again and are now as great as they were in the early part of the last century.[37] Voters have recognized these growing differences. As Figure 5.3 indicates, the percentage of the electorate who perceive a difference between the parties on economic issues grew from 50 percent in 1960 to 78 percent in 2004.[38]

CLASS DIVISIONS IN AMERICAN POLITICS

Given the variations over time in income inequality and party differences on economic issues, we should expect to see relatively greater class divisions in voting behavior prior to the 1950s and again after the 1970s. To assess this possibility, we need individual-level income and voting data covering a long time span. There are two data sources for such an analysis: the Gallup Poll for the 1930s and 1940s, and the American National Election Studies for each election year since 1948. While the surveys themselves differ over time, both sets of data are reputable and allow us to make a *rough* assessment of long-term patterns in the political relevance of class divisions.

In the Gallup polls conducted in 1936 and 1940, respondents were not asked about their income, but interviewers classified people into four categories of affluence on the basis of housing, telephone and car ownership, and the like: "average plus," "average," "poor plus" and "poor."[39] The ANES surveys ask respondents their family income. Respondents are presented with income categories, with small increments between categories, and asked to place themselves in a category. Based on these responses, individuals in the 1948–2004 cumulative ANES data file may be classified by their relative position (percentile) in that year's income distribution.

The ANES cumulative file classifies respondents by income using five percentile categories each year. The percentile groupings are: 0–16, 17–34, 35–62, 63–95, and 95–100. Those in a particular percentile grouping may make more in real dollars in 2000 than in 1980, but our concern is their *relative* economic situation in any given year. With that caveat in mind, respondents in the bottom two percentile groupings are coded together as "lower income" (they account for the bottom third of American wage earners), while those in the top two percentile groupings are coded together to represent those in the top third of family income recipients. The extent of class division is then measured by determining the percentage of those in the lower third who vote Democratic[40] and subtracting from that number the percentage in the top third who vote Democratic. The difference is expressed as the simple measure of difference in percentage points, as is done with other analyses of class divisions.[41]

To assess the long-term relationship between income inequality and class divisions at the polls, Figure 5.4 presents the Gini index (multiplied by 100 to make it comparable to percentages) and the difference between the

FIGURE 5.4 INEQUALITY IN THE DISTRIBUTION OF INCOME, AND CLASS POLITICAL DIVISIONS, 1932 TO 2004

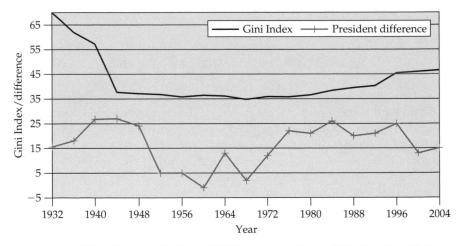

Sources: Robert D. Plotnick, Eugene Smolensky, Eirik Evenjouse, and Siobhan Reilly, "The Twentieth Century Record of Inequality and Poverty in the United States," Institute for Research on Poverty, Discussion Paper no. 1166–98, July, 1998: http://www.irp.wisc.edu/publications/dps/pdfs/dp116698.pdf; and, U.S. Census Bureau: http://www.census.gov/hhes/www/income/histinc/ineqtoc.html; and NES Cumulative File, 1948–2004.

top and bottom thirds of American wage earners in voting for Democratic presidential candidates since 1932. The pattern from 1932 until the 1960s *roughly* squares with conventional wisdom. During the early years of this time span, income inequality was high and class divisions in voting behavior also were relatively high. Through the 1950s and 1960s, inequality declined, as did class divisions at the polls (relative to the levels that prevailed in the 1930s and 1940s). Since 1970, both divisions have increased to the levels that existed in the 1940s, although they declined somewhat in the 2000 and 2004 elections. Roughly speaking, Figure 5.4 shows that class divisions in voting behavior have grown as income inequality has increased.[42]

Figure 5.5 presents data on trends since the 1950s using just ANES data and including differences for congressional elections, which clarifies the post–World War II pattern. With inequality growing, the parties diverging in their electoral bases and concerns,[43] and regionalism declining,[44] it became possible for political divisions revolving around class to emerge.[45] In the 1950s and 1960s, there were limited political differences between the bottom and top income thirds. Beginning in the 1970s, these differences began to increase. This difference increased further in the 1980s and 1990s[46] and then declined in 2000 and 2004.[47]

FIGURE 5.5 INEQUALITY AND CLASS POLITICAL DIVISIONS, 1952 TO 2004

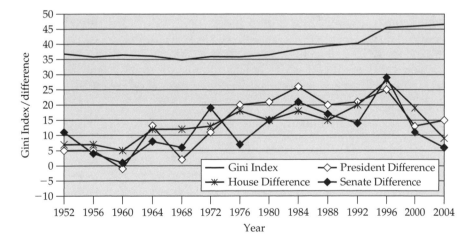

Sources: Robert D. Plotnick, Eugene Smolensky, Eirik Evenjouse, and Siobhan Reilly, "The Twentieth Century Record of Inequality and Poverty in the United States," Institute for Research on Poverty, Discussion Paper no. 1166–98, July, 1998: http://www.irp.wisc.edu/publications/dps/pdfs/dp116698.pdf; and, U.S. Census Bureau: http://www.census.gov/hhes/www/income/histinc/ineqtoc.html; and NES Cumulative File, 1948–2004.

CONSTRAINTS ON CLASS DIVISIONS

The decline in the political significance of class divisions in the last two presidential elections is puzzling, since inequality and party polarization have continued to grow. Our explanation for this puzzle is that short-term, election-specific factors are the likely source of the recent shrinking of the class gap at the polls. There is much analysis to do to understand these two elections, but two factors are of special importance. In 2000, it is likely that many voters did not recognize just how conservative George W. Bush would be as president. As a candidate in 2000, Bush presented himself as a "compassionate conservative," suggesting that he might have some of the same moderate inclinations as his father, who promised a "kinder and gentler" administration when he became president in 1988. In 2000, Bush also was a vigorous advocate of the "No Child Left Behind" program, which sounded vaguely like a liberal program to help students in poorer school districts. The image created by these campaign themes undoubtedly diminished the public's perception of him as a staunch conservative. As Figure 5.3 indicates, there was no increase in the percentage of Americans who saw a difference between the two parties on economic issues in 2000. Four years later, however, there was a significant increase—once Americans realized just how conservative Bush actually is.

In 2004, the war in Iraq relegated most other political issues to secondary status. The issue powerfully divided the electorate, overwhelming most other sources of political division. Table 5.1 indicates the impact of opinions about Iraq on presidential and House voting in 2004. Approval and disapproval of the war created splits within income groups of almost 70 percentage points. Only 10.5 percent of lower-income Americans who supported the war voted for Kerry, while 79.6 percent of lower-income Americans who disapproved of the war supported Kerry. The same split was present among those with higher incomes. There was still a modest overall division by income level in

TABLE 5.1   THE 2004 ELECTION, THE WAR IN IRAQ, AND CLASS DIVISIONS

			PERCENTAGE VOTING DEMOCRATIC BY:			
			APPROVE OF BUSH IRAQ POLICY		DISAPPROVE OF BUSH IRAQ POLICY	
INCOME	PRESIDENT	HOUSE	PRESIDENT	HOUSE	PRESIDENT	HOUSE
Lower	57.1	58.5	10.5	32.9	79.6	72.3
Middle	48.5	53.1	10.7	21.8	77.3	76.4
Higher	41.4	47.6	1.1	10.4	72.2	72.8

Source: Data from the 2004 American National Election Study.

congressional and presidential voting, but it was diminished compared to the prior two decades because of the strong impact of opinions about the war. It is noteworthy that the same sort of split occurred in 1998 around the issue of impeachment, reducing class divisions in that election cycle as well.[48] While the broad social trend of growing inequality and growing differences between the parties may create the potential for a significant class division at the polls, powerful short-term issues such as war or impeachment can push that potential aside.

CULTURE WARS AND CLASS DIVISIONS

Another potential, and perhaps longer-term, constraint on class divisions has been the growing prominence of socio-moral issues in American politics.[49] Just as they have diverged since the late 1970s around economic issues, the Republican and Democratic parties also have taken widely divergent stances on socio-moral issues. While both sets of issues play a prominent role in defining parties' positions and activities, much of the attention in recent years has been on how the emergence of socio-moral issues has displaced economic issues and suppressed class divisions.[50] Presumably, the less affluent have grown more concerned about socio-moral issues and defected from the Democratic Party as a result.[51]

The "culture wars thesis" is a scholarly argument that the United States increasingly is divided between two starkly different points of view regarding socio-moral issues. Traditionalists believe in the existence of an objective moral order and see religious teachings as the ultimate source of authority. Modernists, on the other hand, typically lack strong religious commitment and believe that morality is individually defined. Instead, they place their faith in science, technology, and social progress. In short, traditionalists and modernists differ in their root understandings of morality and the appropriate role of the state in furthering moral standards.[52] Each group's understanding of the moral order leads to different ideas about which identities and behaviors are acceptable in society. Traditionalists and modernists differ in their reaction to and support for teaching creationism in public schools, conducting stem cell research, tolerating homosexuality, and allowing euthanasia, among many other policy differences.[53] The two major political parties have shaped their platforms in accordance with these cultural divisions.

The important matter for this analysis is the effect these "culture wars" may have had on class divisions. Some scholars argue that the Republicans have used socio-moral issues to appeal to working-class Whites who are more supportive of traditional norms and values.[54] The idea is that the Republicans build an unlikely coalition of affluent Americans who prefer

small government and the culturally conservative working class,[55] which
has had the effect of diminishing the political relevance of class divisions.
The presumption of such analyses is that Republicans can retain the support of the more affluent by pushing for tax cuts and fewer government regulations while simultaneously increasing their support among the less
affluent by stressing culture wars issues.[56] While this argument has gained
credibility, it neglects the possibility that as the Republican Party advocates
cultural conservatism, it actually may be alienating the more affluent. If this
is true, we may see a diminishment of class divisions in American politics,
but for quite different reasons than those discussed above.

   While Republicans have pushed relentlessly for tax cuts that provide
significant benefits to affluent Americans, the top third of the income distribution has steadily reduced its support for Republican candidates since
1980. Figure 5.6 presents the trends for income groups in support of Democratic presidential candidates since 1976. The least affluent (those in the bottom third) have not moved away from the Democratic Party, and voters in
the top third have become more Democratic. What is particularly puzzling
is what has happened following each recent Republican presidential administration. Holding the White House allows a party to highlight its positions
to the electorate, thereby attracting (or repelling) specific groups of voters.
Since 1980, the percentage of the more affluent voting for Democratic presidential candidates has increased following each successive Republican
administration. While most scholarly focus has been on the voting behavior
of the less affluent, it is the behavior of the most affluent that evidently needs
to be explained. The issue is whether the culture wars play a role in explaining this increasingly Democratic trend in the voting behavior of the most
affluent American citizens.

FIGURE 5.6   PERCENT VOTING DEMOCRATIC BY INCOME GROUP

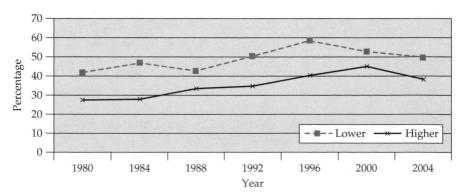

Source: NES Cumulative File, 1948–2004.

INCOME AND ABORTION VIEWS

The culture wars encompass many issues, but perhaps none is more politically potent than abortion.[57] Abortion embodies the essence of cultural conflict because it produces two distinctive and irreconcilable discourses: the "culture of life versus culture of death" discourse (as Pope John Paul II famously articulated it) and the privacy/women's rights discourse.[58] These two discourses involve entirely different values and symbols.[59] The abortion issue has become a significant source of difference between the two parties and a highly effective means of attracting and mobilizing various constituencies.[60] The Democratic Party's commitment to women's reproductive rights since 1972 has led Democratic candidates to do especially well among many women and cultural progressives. Meanwhile, Republicans have stressed their opposition to abortion, which has brought them the support of many formerly Democratic constituencies, including southerners, residents of rural areas, evangelical Protestants, and traditional Catholics.[61]

The question is whether pro-life sentiment is stronger among the less affluent—and perhaps capable of diminishing their support for the Democrats. The evidence indicates that as income rises, so does support for abortion rights.[62] Voters of higher socioeconomic status are more likely to favor legal abortion than are voters of lower socioeconomic status.[63] The positive relationship between abortion attitudes and income is attributable, at least in part, to the correlation between education and income. As educational attainment increases, so does tolerance for abortion rights,[64] because education exposes individuals to alternative worldviews and encourages critical thought.[65] In this sense, education has a liberalizing effect on abortion views.[66] Higher-income voters are thus statistically more likely to embrace less absolute, modernist views on socio-moral issues.

Figure 5.7 confirms this divergence in abortion opinion by income level[67] using ANES data. Pro-choice views are defined here as believing that at a minimum, abortion should be allowed in most circumstances. We find that the least wealthy citizens (those in the bottom third) are consistently more pro-life than wealthier individuals. Meanwhile, America's wealthiest citizens have grown more supportive of abortion rights over the past 30 years. By 2000, almost two-thirds of those in the wealthiest third of the American population were pro-choice.

Does their pro-life position on abortion have the effect of pulling lower-income Americans away from the Democratic Party? It goes without saying that the parties differ over abortion. In the past two decades, party positions on the abortion issue have become even clearer and more divergent,[68] and the issue has come to play a greater role in voting decisions.[69] Abortion by itself could be making lower-income voters more Republican.

There are two different ways in which abortion might shape class-based electoral gaps. If the least affluent are more pro-life—and strongly motivated by

FIGURE 5.7   INCOME AND PRO-CHOICE ABORTION VIEWS

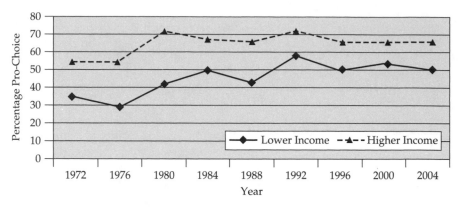

Source: NES Cumulative File, 1948–2004.

this particular issue—then we should expect them to defect from the Democratic Party, reducing the overall class division in the electorate. At the same time, the most affluent—who are primarily pro-choice—may defect from the Republicans over the abortion issue, also reducing the size of class divisions in voting behavior.

What we must now determine is how abortion views affect the voting behavior of specific income groups. How do pro-life and pro-choice voters in different income categories differ in their political behavior? For some Americans, income level and abortion opinions have mutually reinforcing effects on voting behavior. Lower-income people with pro-choice views would be drawn to the Democratic Party on both counts. Likewise, higher-income, pro-life individuals would be in agreement with the Republican Party on both accords.

On the other hand, many Americans are "cross-pressured" because their abortion views clash with those of the party with which they would be likely to affiliate on the basis of their social class. Have lower-income individuals with pro-life opinions moved away from the Democratic Party? Have pro-choice people who earn large incomes become less Republican? Either of these developments should be expected to result in a diminishment of class divisions in the electorate.

Figure 5.8 tracks Democratic voting in presidential elections since 1980, when the abortion issue began to be especially relevant, for those with reinforced views (lower-income, pro-choice voters and higher-income, pro-life voters). The trends fit our expectations, as outlined above: the combination of class and abortion views *does* push these voters farther apart over time. During the period shown in Figure 5.8, both class-related and socio-moral concerns became more politically salient, and abortion opinions reinforced existing class divisions.

Even more central to our analysis are the results shown in Figure 5.9 concerning cross-pressured voters. If the Democratic Party's position on abortion

FIGURE 5.8   REINFORCING CLASS: PERCENT VOTING DEMOCRATIC FOR THOSE
WITH REINFORCED VIEWS

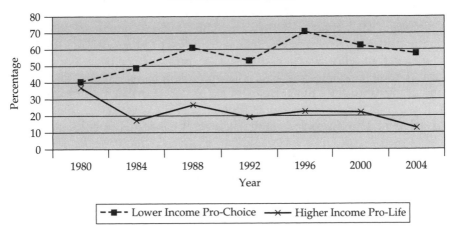

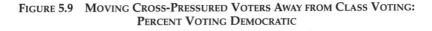

Source: NES Cumulative File, 1948–2004.

has alienated less-affluent people who hold pro-life views, we should observe
them moving away from the Democratic Party. Likewise, if the abortion position of the Republican Party has alienated more affluent, pro-choice voters, we
would expect to find them moving away from the Republican Party.

As Figure 5.9 shows, however, there has been almost *no* movement of the
lower-income, pro-life group away from the Democratic Party over the last
quarter century. In 1980, 43.7 percent of this group voted Democratic; in 2004,
41.0 percent voted Democratic. These cross-pressured voters are less supportive of Democrats than are lower-income, pro-choice voters, but they have
not moved en masse to the Republican Party.

FIGURE 5.9   MOVING CROSS-PRESSURED VOTERS AWAY FROM CLASS VOTING:
PERCENT VOTING DEMOCRATIC

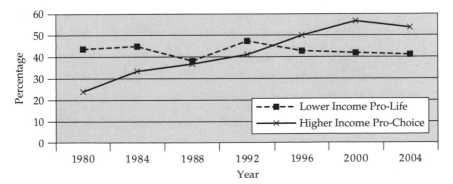

Source: NES Cumulative File, 1948–2004.

The political changes that have transpired since 1980 among the most affluent Americans are especially remarkable. In 1980, pro-life affluent Americans voted more Democratic (46.7 percent) than did pro-choice affluent Americans (23.8 percent). As the issue of abortion became more salient and Republicans became clearly associated with the pro-life position, however, pro-life affluent voters' support of the Democrats declined by 23.9 percentage points. Simultaneously, pro-choice affluent voters increased their support of Democratic candidates by 30.1 percentage points. Further, in both 2000 and 2004, over 60 percent of the most affluent Americans were pro-choice—and this subset of Americans votes more Democratic than Republican.

CONCLUSION

As we have seen, American class divisions—and their political significance—have grown since the 1970s, but 2000 and 2004 bucked this trend. While the conventional argument is that the class division declined because the White working class moved away from the Democratic Party over socio-moral issues such as abortion, our evidence does not support such a conclusion. Over the last three decades, as abortion became especially politically salient, less-affluent pro-life voters have *not* deserted the Democratic Party. They may have lagged behind less-affluent pro-choice voters in that they did not *increase* their support for the Democratic Party, but neither have they moved away from it. On the whole, twin trends of support for abortion rights and support for the Democratic Party have kept the least affluent Americans solidly in the Democratic camp. In the 1970s, the least affluent Americans (those in the bottom third) cast 42.7 percent of their votes on average for Democratic candidates. In the 1980s, this figure rose slightly to 43.6 percent. By the 1990s, the average had grown to 54.2 percent, and in the 2000s it has been 50.9 percent. Even with the dip we have witnessed in the 2000s, the least affluent Americans are still far more supportive of the Democrats today than they were as recently as the 1980s.

The political changes we see among the most affluent citizens over the same time period have been equally fascinating. We find that their partisan support depends heavily on their abortion views. Since a majority of affluent voters are now pro-choice, the net effect has been an increase over time in their support for Democratic candidates. Among Whites in the top third of the income distribution, the average level of support for Democratic candidates in the 1970s was 33.4 percent, and in the 1980s it was 29.7 percent. By the 1990s, however, it had grown to 37.7 percent, and in the 2000s it has been 41.5 percent.

The Republicans' embrace of the pro-life position clearly has mobilized social conservatives to support the party. That policy position, however, also has had some negative consequences for the Republicans. While the party consistently has advocated and enacted tax policies that provide significant benefits for the affluent, those policies have not been sufficient enough to offset the negative effects of the party's position on abortion. As the noted political observer E. J. Dionne has argued, maintaining a coalition of those who desire less government intrusion with those who wish the government to regulate morality is a difficult balancing act at best.[70] The trend of partisan voting by the more affluent over the last 30 years indicates just how difficult that challenge actually is.

The net effect of these trends is that the class divisions that might have grown steadily instead have been somewhat constrained. That constraint has not occurred because Republicans have been able to attract the less affluent, but because they are alienating many of the more affluent. If the Republicans continue to oppose gay rights, stem cell research, and the teaching of evolution, they will likely continue to lose the support of America's most affluent voters.

How will each party handle class issues in the future? Will Democrats shy away from class-related issues or make them more central and seek even greater support from the less affluent? If they pursue the latter strategy, do not be surprised to find class divisions becoming increasingly relevant in American politics. Will Republicans notice the decline in support among the more affluent and temper their positions on socio-moral issues, or will they perceive their cultural conservative base as the most reliable source of votes and thus continue to stress values issues? The decisions party leaders make in answering these questions will shape the future of class-based divisions in American politics.

NOTES

[1]Jennifer L. Hochschild, *Facing Up to the American Dream: Race, Class, and the Soul of the Nation* (Princeton, NJ: Princeton University Press, 1995).

[2]Dan Baltz, "Democrats Assessing the New Climate," *Washington Post* (July 29, 2002): A4.

[3]Terry Bimes and Quinn Mulroy, "The Rise and Decline of Presidential Populism," *Studies in American Political Development* 18 (2004): 136–159.

[4]John B. Judis and Ruy Teixeira, "Why Democrats Must Be Populists," *The American Prospect* 13 (2002): 25–28.

[5]Daniel Bell, *The End of Ideology* (New York: Collier, 1962).

[6]Ronald Inglehart, "The Silent Revolution in Europe," *American Political Science Review* 65 (1971): 991–1017; Ronald Inglehart, *Silent Revolution* (Princeton, NJ: Princeton University Press, 1977); Ronald Inglehart, *Culture Shift in Advanced Industrial Society* (Princeton, NJ: Princeton University Press). See also Everett Carll Ladd and Charles Hadley, *Transformations of the American Party System*, 2nd ed. (New York: W.W. Norton, 1978).

[7]Edward G. Carmines and James Stimson, *Issue Evolution: Race and the Transformation of American Politics* (Princeton, NJ: Princeton University Press, 1989); Thomas Byrne Edsall and Mary D. Edsall, *Chain Reaction: The Impact of Race, Rights, and Taxes on American Politics* (New York: W.W. Norton, 1991): 137–153.

[8]Robert Huckfeldt and Carol W. Kohfeld, *Race and the Decline of Class in American Politics* (Urbana: University of Illinois Press, 1989): 6–16.

[9]V. O. Key, Jr., *Southern Politics in State and Nation* (New York: Knopf, 1949).

[10]Ben J. Wattenberg, *Values Matter Most* (Washington, DC: Regnery, 1995).

[11]Ladd and Hadley (1978): 27.

[12]Robert R. Alford, *Party and Society: The Anglo-American Democracies* (Westport, CT: Greenwood Press, 1963); William H. Flanigan and Nancy H. Zingale, *Political Behavior of the American Electorate*, 8th ed. (Washington, DC: CQ Press, 1994).

[13]Regarding self-identity, respondents in ANES surveys were presented with a question of whether they regarded themselves as middle or working class. For socioeconomic status, respondents were classified based on a combination of their income, education, and occupation. See Ladd and Hadley (1978).

[14]Inglehart (1971); Ladd and Hadley (1978): 73, 195–200, 233–239.

[15]Paul R. Abramson, "Generational Change in American Electoral Behavior," *American Political Science Review* 68 (1974): 102–105; Paul R. Abramson, John H. Aldrich, and David W. Rohde, *Change and Continuity in the 1992 Elections* (Washington, DC: CQ Press, 1995): 146, 152–153; Paul Allen Beck and Frank J. Sorauf, *Party Politics in America*, 7th ed. (New York: HarperCollins, 1992): 166; John W. Brooks and JoAnn B. Reynolds, "A Note on Class Voting in Great Britain and the United States," *Comparative Political Studies* 8 (1975): 368; Edward G. Carmines and Harold W. Stanley, "The Transformation of the New Deal Party System: Social Groups, Political Ideology, and Changing Partisanship among Northern Whites, 1972–1988," *Political Behavior* 14 (1992): 221–222; Edsall and Edsall (1991): 104; Flanigan and Zingale (1994): 104–105; Norvall Glenn, "Class and Party Support in the United States: Recent and Emerging Trends," *Public Opinion Quarterly* 37 (1972): 31–47; William J. Keefe, *Parties, Politics, and Public Policy in America* (Washington, DC: CQ Press, 1994): 214; Everett Carll Ladd, "The Shifting Party Coalitions, 1932–1976," in *Emerging Coalitions in American Politics*, ed. Seymour Martin Lipset (San Francisco: Institute for Contemporary Studies, 1978): 98; Everett Carll Ladd, "Political Parties and Presidential Elections in the Postindustrial Era," in *American Presidential Elections*, ed. Harvey L. Schantz (Albany: State University of New York Press, 1996): 204–206; David G. Lawrence, *The Collapse of the Democratic Presidential Majority* (Boulder, CO: Westview, 1997): 40; Harold W. Stanley and Richard G. Niemi, "The Demise of the New Deal Coalition: Partisanship and Group Support, 1952–1992," in *Democracy's Feast: Elections in America*, ed. Herbert F. Weisberg (Chatham, MA: Chatham House, 1995): 237; Richard J. Trilling, *Party Image and Electoral Behavior* (New York: John Wiley, 1976): 95–130.

[16]John H. Aldrich and Richard G. Niemi, "The Sixth American Party System: Electoral Change, 1952–1992," in *The Broken Contract: Changing Relationships Between Americans and Their Government* (Boulder, CO: Westview, 1996): 87–109; Edward G. Carmines and Geoffrey C. Layman, "Issue Evolution in Postwar American Politics: Old Certainties and Fresh Tension," in *Present Discontents*, ed. Byron E. Shafer (Chatham, MA: Chatham Publishers, 1997a); Edward G. Carmines and Geoffrey C. Layman, "Value Priorities, Partisanship, and Electoral Choice: The Neglected Case of the United States," *Political Behavior* 19 (1997b): 283–316.

[17]James Davison Hunter, *Culture Wars: The Struggle to Define America* (New York: Basic Books, 1991).

[18]Mark D. Brewer and Jeffrey M. Stonecash, *Split: Class and Cultural Divisions in American Politics* (Washington, DC: CQ Press, 2006): 87–162.

[19]Hunter (1991): 63.

[20]Thomas Frank, *What's the Matter with Kansas? How Conservatives Won the Heart of America* (New York: Metropolitan Books, 2004): 105.

[21]The approaches that were used to measure class had reasonable logics. Those following the Marxian tradition focused on whether a worker was in a nonmanual or manual job (Alford, 1963: 79–81). Others conceived of class as a composite of indicators of socioeconomic status, combining income, education, and occupation: see Ladd and Hadley (1975): 64–74; John R. Petrocik, *Party Coalitions: Realignments and the Decline of the New Deal Party System* (Chicago: University of Chicago Press, 1981): 172–173. These seemingly objective indicators drew criticism on the grounds that they did not recognize the importance of the class-consciousness or self-location of respondents in the society. To place the emphasis on how people see themselves, surveys in the 1940s began to ask people whether they regarded themselves as middle or working class: see Abramson, Aldrich, and Rohde (1995): 153; Mary Jackman and Robert Jackman, *Class Awareness in the United States* (Berkeley: University of California Press, 1983). Each of these measures has drawbacks. The manual/nonmanual distinction, while perhaps

once a useful division, does little to capture the enormous variations in economic situations for people with nonmanual jobs in a complex economy: see Clem Brooks and Jeff Manza, "Class Politics and Political Change in the United States, 1952–1992," *Social Forces* 76 (1997a): 379–408; Clem Brooks and Jeff Manza, "Social Cleavages and Political Alignments: U.S. Presidential Elections, 1960-1992," *American Sociological Review* 62 (1997b): 191–208. The socioeconomic indicators, which incorporate education and occupation, measure status as much as economic position. Status involves notions of the value or respect accorded to some position, but status is quite different from relative economic situation: see David R. Segal and David Knoke, "Class Inconsistency, Status Inconsistency, and Partisanship in the United States," *Journal of Politics* 33 (1971): 942. Self-identified class, while valuable as a reflection of self-perceived status, also does not specifically track economic location.

[22]Jeffrey M. Stonecash, *Class and Party in American Politics* (Boulder, CO: Westview, 2000).

[23]Nolan McCarty, Keith T. Poole, and Howard L. Rosenthal, *Polarized America: The Dance of Ideology and Unequal Riches* (Cambridge, MA: MIT Press, 2006).

[24]Jeffrey M. Stonecash, "Class Divisions in American Politics," *PS: Political Science and Politics* 39 (2006a): 461–465.

[25]Lisa Keister, *Wealth in America* (New York: Cambridge University Press, 2000).

[26]Sheldon Danziger and Peter Gottschalk, *America Unequal* (Cambridge, MA: Harvard University Press, 1995): 53.

[27]Danziger and Gottschalk (1995): 76–81; Howard V. Hayghe, "Developments in Women's Labor Force Participation," *Monthly Labor Review* (September 1997): 42.

[28]Louis Uchitelle, "Job Growth Falters in Possible Sign that Economy Is Starting to Slow," *New York Times* (October 9, 1999): C1.

[29]Isaac Shapiro, Robert Greenstein, and Wendell Primus, "Pathbreaking CBO Study Shows Dramatic Increases in Income Disparities in 1980s and 1990s," *Center on Budget and Policy Priorities* (Washington, DC, May 31, 2001): 10.

[30]See Robert D. Plotnick, Eugene Smolensky, Eirik Evenhouse, and Siobhan Reilly, "The Twentieth Century Record of Inequality and Poverty in the United States," University of Wisconsin-Madison Institute for Research on Poverty Discussion Paper no. 1166–98 (1998). The logic of the Gini index is to set perfect equality as a baseline and then measure divergence from that point. If every one percent of the population had one percent of the total national income, we would have perfect equality. If we were to plot this geometrically, every percentage increase in the percentage of the population would be matched by an equivalent percentage of income. In contrast, if there is inequality and 50 percent of the population earns only 25 percent of the income, a discrepancy from that baseline develops. The greater this discrepancy, the greater the inequality, and the higher the value of the Gini index. The index runs from 0 to 1. A score of zero indicates there is no difference between the percentage of the population and the percentage of income received by that population. High scores indicate that a small percentage of the population earns a large percentage of the income. Plotnick et al. (1998) use the Gini index for family incomes from the Bureau of the Census for 1947–1996. To estimate scores for 1913–1964, they first fit an equation to estimate the Gini index for 1947–1996 using several independent variables. They proceed to use the parameters derived from the 1947–1996 equation results and data on the same independent variables from 1913–1946 to estimate a Gini index for 1913–1946. The Gini index from 1997–2004 is taken from U.S. Census Bureau Historical Income Tables, available at http://www.census.gov/hhes/www/income/histinc/ie1.html.

[31]Brewer and Stonecash (2006): Chapter 3.

[32]Alan I. Abramowitz and Kyle L. Saunders, "Ideological Realignments in the U.S. Electorate," *Journal of Politics* 60 (1998): 634–652; E. J. Dionne, Jr., *They Only Look Dead* (New York: Touchstone, 1996); John Gerring, *Party Ideologies in America* (New York: Cambridge University Press, 1998); Gary C. Jacobson, "Party Polarization in National Politics: The Electoral Connection," in *Polarized Politics*, eds. Jon R. Bond and Richard Fleisher (Washington, DC: CQ Press, 2000): 9–30; Gary C. Jacobson, "Party Polarization in Presidential Support: The Electoral Connection," *Congress and the Presidency* 30 (2003): 1–36.

[33]Robert S. Erikson and Gerald C. Wright, "Voters, Issues, and Candidates in Congressional Elections," in *Congress Reconsidered*, 7th ed., eds. Lawrence Dodd and Bruce Oppenheimer (Washington, DC: CQ Press, 2001): 74–76; Stonecash (2000).

[34]Tim Groseclose, Steven D. Levitt, and James M. Snyder, Jr., "Comparing Interest Group Scores across Time and Chambers: Adjusted ADA Scores for the U.S. Congress," *American Political Science Review* 93 (1999): 33–50; Jacobson (2003).

[35]Keith T. Poole and Howard L. Rosenthal, *Ideology and Congress* (New Brunswick, NJ: Transaction, 2007).

[36]McCarty, Poole, and Rosenthal (2006); Jeffrey M. Stonecash, Mark D. Brewer, and Mack D. Mariani, *Diverging Parties: Social Change, Realignment, and Party Polarization* (Boulder, CO: Westview, 2003).

[37]Brewer and Stonecash (2006): 41–65; Gerring (1998): 125–158, 232–253; Gary C. Jacobson, *A Uniter, Not a Divider?* (New York: Longman, 2006); Jeffrey M. Stonecash, *Parties Matter: Realignment and the Return of Partisanship* (Boulder, CO: Lynne Rienner, 2006b); Andrew J. Taylor, "The Ideological Development of the Parties in Washington, 1947–1994," *Polity* 39 (1996): 273–292.

[38]John H. Aldrich, *Why Parties?* (Chicago: University of Chicago Press, 1995).

[39]Ladd and Hadley (1978): 53. I do not know the specific instructions that interviewers were given in classifying respondents. I acquired the data files and codebooks for the polls conducted by the Gallup Organization during the 1930s and the 1940s. The first poll was done in October 1936, and asks only about the presidential election. Those participating in interviews in 1936 were classified as "average plus," "average," "poor or poor plus," or "on relief." (The distribution of this classification roughly accords with data in the ANES cumulative file.) Of those who are classified, 35.9 percent are in the category of "average plus"; 27.6 percent are in the "average" category; 36.5 percent are in the "poor plus," "poor," or "on relief" categories. In a 1940 Gallup Poll, the category "wealthy" was added. Of those who were classified in 1940, 43.7 percent are in the categories of "wealthy," "average plus," and "average," while 19.2 percent are in the "poor" category and 36.9 percent are in the "poor plus" or "on relief" categories. For 1940, if we combine the "wealthy" and "average plus" categories, they constitute only 13.4 percent of respondents. Calculating the political division between the more affluent and the bottom 36.9 percent reveals a much greater gap (a 46-point difference rather than the 26.8-point difference that emerges if the top 43.7 percent of wage earners are compared to the bottom 36.9 percent). I chose to contrast the larger groupings and therefore use the 26.8-point difference. Regardless, the differences in the 1930s and the 1940s were much greater than they were in the 1950s and 1960s.

[40]The 1932 presidential results are taken from the October 1936 poll and should be viewed with some caution. Respondents were asked whom they voted for in 1932. There are, of course, problems of recall, not to mention the fact that individuals may have experienced considerable economic change between 1932 and 1936 such that their 1936 financial situation did not reflect their 1932 financial situation, making the cross-tabulation of their 1936 economic situation with the recall of their 1932 vote problematic. With those cautions in mind, the results are still of crude value to indicate the divisions that prevailed in the 1930s relative to later time periods. For readers who are surprised that the class divisions were not greater in 1932, the results indicate that every economic stratum in the American electorate supported Roosevelt—even the most affluent.

[41]More complete analyses of post–World War II changes in class divisions are presented in Mark D. Brewer and Jeffrey M. Stonecash, "Class, Race Issues, Declining White Support for the Democratic Party in the South," *Political Behavior* 23 (2001): 131–155; Stonecash (2000); Jeffrey M. Stonecash, Mark D. Brewer, Mary P. McGuire, R. Eric Petersen, and Lori Beth Way, "Class and Party: Secular Realignment and the Survival of Democrats outside the South," *Political Research Quarterly* 53 (2000): 731–752; Stonecash, Brewer, and Mariani (2003).

[42]McCarty, Poole, and Rosenthal (2006).

[43]Jacobson (2003); Stonecash, Brewer, and Mariani (2003).

[44]Stonecash (2006b).

[45]Brewer and Stonecash (2006); Stonecash (2000).

[46]Stonecash (2000).

[47]Stonecash (2006a).

[48]In 1998 there was a significant division revolving around whether Bill Clinton should have been impeached. The intensity of public opinion about this issue was so strong that it dominated voting irrespective of class: see Stonecash (2000): 119–120. Those who supported impeachment voted strongly Republican across class groupings, while those who opposed

it voted strongly Democratic across class groupings. The result was that class divisions were much less prevalent in 1998 than they had been in previous years.

[49]Fiorina (2005).

[50]Hunter (1991); Geoffrey Layman, *The Great Divide* (New York: Columbia University Press, 2001).

[51]Frank (2004).

[52]David C. Leege, Kenneth D. Wald, Brian Krueger, and Paul D. Mueller, *The Politics of Cultural Differences: Social Change and Voter Mobilization Strategies in the Post–New Deal Period* (Princeton, NJ: Princeton University Press, 2002): 41–44.

[53]Ibid., 26.

[54]Frank (2004); Hunter (1991): 63.

[55]Dionne (1996).

[56]Frank (2004).

[57]Alan I. Abramowitz, "It's Abortion, Stupid: Policy Voting in the 1992 Presidential Election," *Journal of Politics* 57 (1995): 176–186; Greg D. Adams, "Abortion: Evidence of an Issue Evolution," *American Journal of Political Science* 41 (1997): 718–737.

[58]Jo Freeman, "Feminism vs. Family Values: Women at the 1992 Democratic and Republican Conventions," *PS: Political Science and Politics* 26 (1993): 21–28.

[59]Murray Edelman, "Political Language and Political Reality," *PS: Political Science and Politics* 18 (1985): 15.

[60]Layman (2001).

[61]Ibid.

[62]Jerome Legge, "The Determinants of Attitudes toward Abortion in the American Electorate," *Western Political Quarterly* 36 (1987): 486.

[63]Abramowitz (1995): 176.

[64]Legge (1987): 480; Guang-zhen Wang and M. Doug Buffalo, "Social and Cultural Determinants of Attitudes toward Abortion: A Test of Reiss' Hypotheses," *Social Science Journal* 43 (2004): 102.

[65]Larry R. Petersen, "Religion, Plausibility Structures, and Education's Effect on Attitudes toward Elective Abortion," *Journal for the Scientific Study of Religion* 40 (2001): 189.

[66]Jerome L. Himmelstein and James A. McRae, Jr., "Social Issues and Socioeconomic Status," *Public Opinion Quarterly* 52 (1988): 500.

[67]For this analysis, only those identifying themselves as White are included. For much of the last 50 years the focus in class analyses has been on Whites. In part that was so because minorities were so overwhelmingly Democratic that whatever class divisions existed washed out, so non-Whites were excluded to get a clearer picture of the political behavior of Whites. Whites were also the focus of much research because a good deal of the commentary about race and cultural issues suggested that the political role of such issues has been to agitate Whites so much that class divisions declined. For example, some have argued that widespread racism among Whites has led all of them to move in the Republican direction. In particular, much of the culture wars commentary has involved a focus on how socio-moral and cultural issues have pulled Whites away from the Democratic Party. For all of these reasons, Whites only are examined in this analysis of the role of abortion.

[68]Adams (1997): 723–724.

[69]Brewer and Stonecash (2006); Elizabeth Adell Cook, Ted G. Jelen, and Clyde Wilcox, "State Political Cultures and Public Opinion about Abortion," *Political Research Quarterly* 46 (1993): 771–781.

[70]Dionne (1996).

6

THE RURAL–URBAN GAP*

❧

JAMES G. GIMPEL
KIMBERLY A. KARNES

R ecent presidential elections have revealed an urban–rural cleavage in voting behavior that is hard to dismiss. Most observers now recognize that
the election night maps showing the "red" states versus the "blue" actually
mask an urban versus rural divide *within* states, a gap that recently has grown
larger than ever. In 2004, the difference in Democratic support between the
most and least populous counties in the United States exceeded 25 points (see
Figure 6.1). Tabulations from the 2000 and 2004 American National Election
Studies indicate a 20-point gap in presidential preference between people who
live in counties with more than a million residents and those who live in counties with populations smaller than 25,000 (see Table 6.1).

Party strategists are alarmed by this gap, particularly those on the Democratic side. Individually, the nation's tiniest burgs do not amount to much. Col-
lectively, however, rural voters routinely deliver many states' electoral votes to
the Republican Party. In the wake of the 2004 election, Democratic National Committee chair Howard Dean is said to have urged his party's elites to study and
address their "rural problem."[1] Surprisingly, political science seems remarkably
ill prepared to undertake the same task. A great deal of research has been undertaken on urban politics, but there is no remotely comparable body of scholarship
on rural populations.[2] In this chapter, we will take up Dr. Dean's charge to seek
a deeper understanding of the rural side of the urban–rural divide.

There are obvious compositional differences that make different kinds of
places politically distinct from one another (see Table 6.1). Areas with low population density may be politically unique simply because of the geographic distribution of population traits and characteristics. Sparsely settled areas stand out

*Previously published as J.G. Gimpel and K.A. Karnes, "The Rural Side of the Urban-Rural Gap." *PS: Political
Science and Politics* 39 (2006): 467–472. Reprinted with the permission of Cambridge University Press.

FIGURE 6.1   DIFFERENCE IN SUPPORT FOR PRESIDENTIAL CANDIDATES, BY COUNTY SIZE

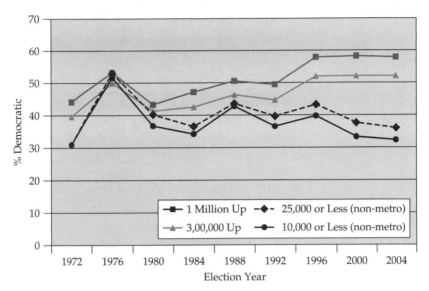

Source: U.S. County population figures from U.S. Census; Presidential vote figures from *America Votes* (Washington, DC: CQ Press, biennial).

from other locations on planet Earth because only certain types of people choose to reside in them. There is nothing magical about place-of-residence, per se, but the peculiar collection of economic and demographic traits of resident populations is the basic ingredient of distinctive rural behaviors and beliefs. Studies reveal that rural voters are, on average, more likely to be White, Christian (and specifically, evangelical), religiously devout, elderly, less educated, and less affluent than voters from urban and suburban populations. Rural voters also own more guns, are more likely to oppose abortion rights, and hew to more traditional family arrangements than those living elsewhere. Urban voters are 18.3 percent more likely than rural voters to label themselves "liberal" (see Table 6.1). Nearly half (49 percent) of rural Americans report attending church at least weekly as compared to just 26 percent of big-city residents. Rural voters are also 10 percent more likely to be apprehensive about the impact of "new lifestyles." Interestingly, one of the biggest gaps shown in Table 6.1 concerns how "wired" the rural and urban populations are. Urban dwellers report far more Internet access than do citizens living in the nation's smallest towns and rural areas. Other distinctive traits of rural Americans, however, are perhaps less obvious.

Rural voters are not more Republican in their party identification than suburban voters, but they are more Republican than the residents of big cities. Nevertheless, there is only a 7 percent difference between rural and urban voters in Republican Party identification and an 8.2 percent difference between urban and rural voters in Democratic Party identification (see Table 6.1). These

TABLE 6.1   THE NATURE OF THE URBAN–RURAL GAP ACROSS POLITICALLY RELEVANT
CHARACTERISTICS OF VOTERS, 2000–2004

	RURAL (<25,000)	OTHER AREAS	URBAN (>1 MILLION)	RURAL/URBAN DIFFERENCE
Bush vote in 2000	62.5% (65)	48.4% (729)	39.2% (148)	+ 23.3%
Turnout in 2000	62.9% (88)	69.4% (1222)	70.7% (313)	− 7.8%
Republican	41.2% (74)	39.5% (1092)	34.2% (197)	+ 7%
Democrat	45.5% (82)	48.1% (1090)	53.7% (309)	− 8.2%
Independent	10.6% (19)	10.6% (240)	11.3% (65)	− 0.7%
Conservative ideology	62.8% (113)	51.1% (1156)	51.1% (294)	+ 11.7%
Liberal ideology	20.0% (36)	33.6% (760)	38.3% (220)	− 18.3%
Income >$100,000	21% (35)	23% (482)	28.9% (153)	− 7.9%
Self-employed	15.6% (28)	12% (272)	12% (69)	3.6%
Own home	76.2% (131)	69.7% (1543)	64.2% (362)	+ 12%
Worship attendance at least weekly	48.8% (63)	36.4% (557)	37% (143)	+ 11.8%
Evangelical	48.9% (88)	30.3% (686)	26.3% (151)	+ 22.6%
Abortion view (pro-choice)	20.0% (33)	40.0% (850)	50.4% (261)	− 30.4%
Welfare spending view (favor decrease)	53.9% (96)	54.3% (1208)	53.2% (298)	+ 0.7%
View on spending for the poor (favor decrease)	19.2% (34)	23.9% (531)	20.2% (114)	− 1%
Concerned about "new lifestyles"	69.4% (104)	63.0% (1244)	59.7% (285)	+ 9.7
View on race ("Blacks could succeed if they tried harder")	65.4% (100)	52.2% (1021)	48.8% (233)	+ 16.6

TABLE 6.1 (CONTINUED)

	RURAL (<25,000)	OTHER AREAS	URBAN (>1 MILLION)	RURAL/URBAN DIFFERENCE
View on affirmative action for Blacks (oppose)	76.3% (116)	83.9% (1663)	81.3% (92)	– 5%
No Internet access	52.9% (82)	34.0% (674)	26.2% (127)	+ 26.7%
Tolerate others' morals	61% (94)	62.6% (1236)	65.8% (314)	– 4.8%
Belief that "we don't give equal chances"	52.6% (80)	46.8% (925)	49.5% (238)	+ 3.1%
View on gun control (not important)	28.3% (51)	29.7% (670)	34.7% (199)	– 6.4%
"We should emphasize traditional values"	90.1% (137)	81.3% (1609)	79.9% (385)	+ 10.2%
N	180	2264	575	

Source: American National Election Studies, 2000 and 2004.

are modest differences, especially when compared to the rural–urban gap in political *ideology*.

Rural Americans are also much more likely to be homeowners and to be self-employed than nonrural residents. Specifically, 76.2 percent of rural respondents own their own homes, compared to 64.2 percent of their urban counterparts. Rural Americans are skeptical of welfare spending, but so are people who live in suburban and urban areas. People who live in rural areas seem more likely than city folk to believe that African Americans could succeed through hard work, but they are not much more opposed than urban residents to affirmative action for African Americans (see Table 6.1). We cannot conclude from these tabulations that people in rural areas are more racist than people in urban areas. Nor can we conclude that all rural Americans predictably believe that individual exertion is all that is needed to overcome disadvantage.

In summary, nearly every credible survey indicates that the voting loyalty of the rural electorate is growing more Republican, while the electorate of the most populous locations is heading in the opposite direction. This trend gives rise to the unmistakable gap shown in Figure 6.1. This gap corresponds to similarly large rural–urban gaps in the inclination to identify oneself as liberal or conservative, in the propensity to adhere to evangelical Protestant religious principles, to oppose abortion rights, and to attend religious services. Smaller but still significant gaps appear around less obvious matters such as home-ownership, Internet access, and party identification. And contrary to hillbilly stereotypes, the rural population is not entirely Southern; 29 percent of the nation's rural voting-age residents reside in Deep South States, with another 21 percent residing in Border States.[3]

URBAN VOTERS AND DEMOCRATIC LOYALTY

From previous studies of urban politics and voting, we have gained a thorough understanding of the reasons why voters in America's largest cities have grown increasingly loyal to the Democrats. Simply put, the Democratic Party is appealing to urban populations because people living in cities are pre-dominantly poor, ethnically diverse, and more liberal on key social issues. Democratic positions favoring aggressive enforcement of civil rights laws, for instance, are attractive to minority populations who contend that they have been victimized by discrimination at the hands of the White majority. Demo-cratic support for policies to promote egalitarian outcomes is attractive to urban populations for the same reason. City dwellers appear to favor efforts to level the societal playing field and diminish the extent of inherited advan-tage and wealth accumulation among the most affluent.

White liberals in affluent city neighborhoods vote Democratic, but they do so for different reasons than their more socioeconomically challenged urban neighbors. For affluent city dwellers, the Democratic Party represents tolerance of less traditional ways of life and support for abortion rights. Democrats are also perceived as being committed to environmental protection, the preser-vation of civil liberties, ending the war in Iraq, and assorted other progressive causes, such as government funding for stem cell research.

By 2000, 20 large American cities had majority Black populations, and 32 more were at least one-third Black. Indeed, by the beginning of the twenty-first century, 80 percent of all African Americans lived in large cities. This influx of Blacks into urban areas where White majorities were once sizable thrust race relations to the forefront of the national policy agenda. With African-American migration to urban areas, White voters often fled to suburbs, leading to the segregation of Black populations inside cities.[4] With the geographic isolation of large African-American populations from economic opportunity in bur-geoning suburbs, residents of Black neighborhoods quickly sank into sustained, long-term poverty.[5] Meanwhile, the twentieth century saw African Americans become a key constituency of the Democratic Party, the party that since the New Deal era had come to best represent the poor and downtrodden.[6]

Well before African Americans began migrating to urban areas, immi-grants from Europe flooded into American cities. Their arrival generated a strong current of ethnic politics, as group identities were formed around ances-tral ties.[7] Immigration continues to have a strong impact on urban politics today. While the ethnically anchored political party machines of a hundred years ago are unlikely to rise again, new waves of immigrants from Latin America and Asia are reshaping city politics, creating new local conflicts and political cleavages.[8] Up until now, Republicans have been unable to exploit these divisions in national politics, although GOP candidates have won a few prominent mayoral contests. Mostly, though, Republicans are widely perceived as having little to offer to urban liberal and minority voters.

The result is a rather heterodox political coalition in big cities for the Democrats when major statewide and national elections are at stake. Affluent residents and those who live in desperate poverty unite in support of Democratic candidates, and the strength of this loyalty has only increased in recent elections (see Figure 6.1). The potential politicization of class divisions between wealthy voters and poor voters has been submerged in favor of an alliance across socioeconomic lines that centers around liberal views on moral and social issues and support for government assistance to promote the betterment of large cities and their underprivileged populations. In American politics, economic differences commonly have been papered over for the sake of maintaining political party unity in regions, states, and localities.[9] That the Democratic electoral coalition in urban areas would contain economically and socially diverse groups makes sense given that the two major political parties must encompass diverse interests. By bundling seemingly contradictory positions together, party leaders hope to package their candidates in a way that will result in majority support.

RURAL VOTERS AND REPUBLICAN LOYALTY

The populations of most rural areas are less racially and economically diverse than the populations of cites. The countryside nevertheless contains interests that would appear to be at odds despite rural voters' strong and consistent support for Republican candidates. For instance, rural Americans are in the bottom quarter of the overall U.S. income distribution, which might constitute grounds for an alliance with socioeconomically challenged city dwellers on issues such as economic redistribution and government intervention in business. At the same time, consistent with their deeply held religious beliefs, the rural electorate is morally and socially conservative on the whole. Rural voters therefore seem to be cross-pressured. They have good reasons to vote with the Democrats on economic matters, but their adherence to traditional family arrangements and acceptance of the role of religion in public life partners them with the Republicans.

Why are rural Americans moving in such a Republican direction when they are economically similar to urban dwellers? It is impossible to ignore Thomas Frank's recent work in this context suggesting that economic vulnerability has been displaced as an issue among rural Americans by the deployment of religious and moral symbols by business-oriented Republican elites.[10] As Frank sees it, the Republican Party's focus on socio-moral issues has distracted "foolish" rural voters away from their legitimate economic grievances and "duped" them into voting with the most affluent Americans. The result has been the formation of a strange coalition on the political right of working-class rural voters and big corporate business interests, with the latter wielding the greater influence. According to this view, rural voters mindlessly participate in the election of candidates who follow the business interests of Wall Street, undermine rural people's own economic position, and give them nothing in return. Frank would posit this logic to explain why some of the poorest rural counties in the United States have given more than 80 percent of their vote to Republican candidates in recent presidential elections.

Geographic divisions in American politics are often anchored in nonpolitical stereotypes about the way people live and think in places that are distant and unfamiliar. Frank's judgment that rural citizens are ill-bred dimwits who vote irrationally will resonate with most metropolitan readers, which is why his argument has been compelling to so many. The unflattering views that urban sophisticates have come to harbor toward rural Americans, and vice versa, have carved out a wide cultural canyon. Those who live in the "bluest" cities apparently believe that rural Americans are dumb, boorish, and bigoted. To be sure, rural Americans also ascribe to some unflattering stereotypes about city folk. Fueled by media coverage from news outlets based primarily in large cities, rural Americans overestimate urban pretension, violence, and moral degeneracy.

But rural Americans' perceptions of city life are, on balance, more accurate than the perceptions urban Americans have of the countryside. This is so because rural citizens are exposed to more information about city life than urban residents are to information about life in rural areas. Rural-to-urban migration and travel is still far more common than urban-to-rural migration. A city dweller's smugness about the superiority of cosmopolitan urban life is constantly reinforced by the media, and fears about venturing beyond the city's confines perpetuates ignorance about life and values elsewhere. Anti-rural biases in education curricula teach youth, rural and urban alike, that the path to success and prosperity is in large cities and suburbs. The worth and future of rural life is perpetually questioned while cities and suburbs are characterized as being forward-thinking.[11]

SOURCES OF URBAN–RURAL DIVISION IN PLACE-BASED STEREOTYPES

The public impression of rural America as a repository of the nation's unwashed masses has a long and colorful history. From the earliest depictions of rural folk in prime-time television series such as *The Beverly Hillbillies, Green Acres, The Andy Griffith Show,* and *Petticoat Junction,* to depictions in more recent reality series such as *The Simple Life* and *Amish in the City,* consistent imagery depicts rural people as being unsophisticated, heavily accented, and semi-literate. They are also frequently depicted working the land, tending livestock, or engaging in related rural occupations, presumably because they are not smart enough to make a living in a big city.[12] The point of *Amish in the City*, according to network executives, was to see what happens to Amish teens "who will walk down Rodeo Drive and be freaked out by what they see."[13] Ironically, the idea that it is acceptable to ridicule the inexperience of a small, rural religious minority apparently raised little ire among people who live in cities that feature numerous programs promoting multiculturalism and tolerance for diversity.

Probably no single offering of American popular culture extended the chasm between urban and rural populations more than the 1972 movie *Deliverance*. This film brings into sharp relief a contrast between urbane professionals out to canoe a river that will soon be dammed to promote development and rustic natives who will be displaced by this modernizing force. To critics, this message is part of a common narrative of economic conquest designed to justify business expansion and modernization at the expense of the less privileged.[14] Regardless of whether this broader claim is true, images from this movie have become a powerful and widely understood cultural reference: rural Americans are not only stupid and ugly, but they are frightening and violent.

A less well-known but critically acclaimed film, *Boys Don't Cry* (1999), clumsily depicts the true story of Teena Brandon, a teenage girl in rural Nebraska who preferred to live as a male, Brandon Teena. The protagonist lives in a small-town world consisting entirely of trailer parks, untended farmhouses, and ex-cons. This film does not acknowledge that Nebraskans do not speak with slow drawls or southern accents. When Brandon's friends discover that she is masquerading as a boy, she is eventually betrayed, humiliated, raped, and murdered. Principal characters are depicted as drunken, criminal, ignorant, vicious, and intolerant. Related depictions of savage "bubbas" in classic films such as *Easy Rider* (1969) and *Pulp Fiction* (1994) also serve to propagate repugnant rural images as they air on cable television on a regular basis.

Few would argue that rural Americans are the only ones who are negatively stereotyped by television and movies. There are many uncomplimentary symbols associated with urban and suburban populations as well. One only need view an episode of ABC's series *Desperate Housewives* to see how Hollywood casts suburban life, or watch the critically acclaimed film *American Beauty* (1999) for a depiction of the supposed depressing dullness of life in suburbia. Images in television and film depicting cities as violent and vice-prone are so numerous that we need not list examples.

With these images shaping the mind-sets of millions of Americans, it is no wonder that polarization by place of residence has made its way into the nation's politics. It has even seemingly supplanted economic interests as a basis for candidate evaluation and group cohesion. Why would we ever think that political identity would remain untouched by the polarized and exaggerated cultural portrayals used to describe places? One may dismiss these differences or pretend that they don't exist, but that will not solve the Democratic Party's "rural problem."

ECONOMIC CHANGE AND THE *EXPERIENCE* OF ECONOMIC CHANGE

Our contention is that the urban–rural divide is rooted in much more than the morality politics discussed above. Frank's argument that rural Americans are easy to fleece politically has been challenged by political scientist Larry Bartels,[15] but not on the grounds articulated here. Bartels soberly insists that Frank's evidence is flawed because economic conditions continue to be important to Americans, regardless of their place of residence. There are several other possible explanations of rural political distinctiveness, however, including: (1) the possibility that economic struggle in rural areas has been exaggerated; (2) the fact that rural self-images are not well understood; and (3) widespread misunderstanding of rural Americans' adaptability to and perceptions of changing economic circumstances.

Perhaps rural Americans are not laboring to choke down their economic misery. This is not so difficult to believe if accounts of rural economic collapse have been exaggerated or if economic conditions and the experience of economic conditions are separable. Republican voting habits may be sustained throughout rural America because it is not so evident to residents that economic conditions have worsened dramatically under Republican leadership more than they did under Democratic leadership, or more than they have in other geographic locations.

In spite of globalization and the move to market-based corporate farming, the sky has not fallen on rural Americans—rather few of whom actually are employed in the agricultural sector. Economic decline in some sectors has been met with improvements in others. The upshot is that rural residents may see little compelling reason to revolt against the Republican Party, at least from a pocketbook perspective.

Studies of life and job satisfaction show that people who live in rural areas are *more* satisfied with their lives and occupations than are those in urban and suburban locations.[16] A good deal of this happiness appears to be anchored in self-employment or an enlarged scope of job responsibility. But even if we control for occupation or self-employment, we must note that key differences in socialization experiences have shaped subjective judgments about the meaning and value of work.[17]

Data from the 2000 American National Election Study indicates that rural residents who work for employers other than themselves were more likely than those living in suburban or urban settings to say they were completely satisfied with their lives (Figure 6.2). Meanwhile, rural residents who were

FIGURE 6.2   LIFE SATISFACTION BY PLACE OF RESIDENCE AND SELF-EMPLOYMENT

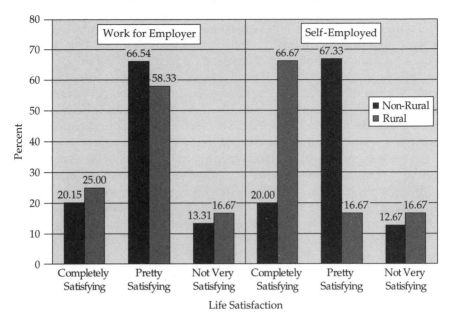

Source: American National Election Study, 2000.

self-employed were far more likely to say they were completely satisfied than self-employed people in nonrural areas (Figure 6.2). Based on this evidence, and many sociological studies addressing life satisfaction, health, and happiness,[18] there is no groundswell of discontent in the remote hinterlands. Maybe the real puzzle is why so many unhappy urban and suburban citizens are not translating *their* high levels of discontent into political demands.

ENTREPRENEURIAL SELF-IMAGES AND PRIVATE PROPERTY

People who live in rural areas are no different than other Americans in the extent to which they discriminate between those who deserve government assistance and those who do not deserve it. In addition, though, rural residents express the same desire as residents of wealthy suburbs for lower taxes, less government regulation of business, and free markets. What explains this apparent paradox?

A strong sense of self-reliance anchored in an individualistic ethic is traceable to the earliest days of the American Republic.[19] This ethic is tied closely to a preference for little or no government regulation of business and a belief in the notion that those who succeed in a competitive marketplace owe nothing to those who fail.[20] Economic individualism shows up not only in the indisputably conservative attitudes of rural Americans toward welfare policy, but is also reinforced by two cornerstone aspects of the rural economy: self-employment and widespread property ownership.

As business owners and homeowners, rural dwellers' commitment to private property thwarts many policy sentiments that might run contrary to an individualistic, competitive ethic. The mode of production that historically has shaped rural areas is that of the small, independent owner-operator—the *petit bourgeois*.[21] There has been little sense of class oppression among rural Americans in contemporary times because of high levels of self-employment and homeownership. According to the 2004 American National Election Study, for example, 3.1 rural residents worked for someone else for every one who reported to be self-employed, but in nonrural areas, this ratio was more than double that: 6.3!

Many rural families own land or other valuable capital items such as buildings, equipment, and store inventories, and are in entrepreneurial control of the allocation of these resources. Moreover, families historically have provided much of the labor in these enterprises themselves, although this tradition is changing with corporate penetration of agriculture and small-town enterprise. Finally, farm and small-business owners naturally operate in a competitive marketplace subject to commodity price shifts, interest rates, and commercial lending practices and regulations. Family farms continue to survive because their reliance on largely unpaid family labor allows them to absorb market downturns that might crush a corporate farm.[22]

The upshot of these economic realities is that many rural voters are comfortable voting Republican because they see themselves as *independent businesspersons* rather than on-the-clock employees. Actual money income plays a relatively small role in their economic evaluations in comparison with self-perceived economic status. As long as these rural owner-operators view their own success as contingent upon market forces, their individualistic beliefs and attitudes will be sustained. No doubt these rural entrepreneurs are not the same types of businesspersons one finds in the boardrooms of corporate America, but they may have more in common with a corporate CEO than they do with an urban service worker or industrial laborer, both of whom pay exorbitant rents for modest housing, punch a time clock, and must ask permission to take a bathroom break, see a physician, or attend a school play.

Survey researchers have suggested that the commitment to self-reliance is somewhat at odds with the value of equality, although the two are not polar opposites.[23] One of the signature facets of rural life is its relative income *equality* typified by a narrow income distribution and a smaller gap between rich and poor than what prevails in metropolitan areas. It is this level aspect of rural life that allows a fierce commitment to individualism to thrive. Rural voters express relatively little systematic concern about the concept of equality in response to survey questions, and this should come as no surprise. Who needs leveling when it exists already?

Table 6.2 illustrates the impact of homeownership and self-employment on the values of egalitarianism and individualism using standard instrumentation from three recent studies. We have controlled for place of residence to evaluate whether it has a separate impact on these core values independent of the general spatial distribution of self-employed persons and homeowners. Controlling for income ensures that homeownership and self-employment are not

TABLE 6.2 THE IMPACT OF SELF-EMPLOYMENT AND HOMEOWNERSHIP ON EGALITARIANISM AND INDIVIDUALISM, BY RURAL OR NONRURAL RESIDENCE, CONTROLLING FOR INCOME

VARIABLE	INDIVIDUALISM 1996–2004[‡]	EGALITARIANISM 1996–2004
Constant	49.728** (2.074)	59.131** (0.967)
Rural resident	–2.571 (2.967)	0.001 (1.381)
Homeowner	3.318** (1.104)	–2.200** (0.530)
Self-employed	8.084** (2.623)	–3.513** (1.215)
Rural x Homeowner	3.404 (3.293)	–2.575* (1.537)
Rural x Self-employed	7.712* (4.617)	–1.882 (2.137)
Highest income (<$105,000)*	13.408** (4.357)	–4.597** (2.056)
Middle income ($35,000–$50,000)	–2.036 (2.422)	–0.078 (1.137)
Low income ($15,000–$30,000)	–9.288** (2.015)	0.555 (0.935)
Lowest income (>$15,000)	–14.601** (1.971)	0.805 (0.914)
N	3265	3382
F	16.596	15.373
p	0.001	0.001
R^2	0.05	0.05

Ordinary Least Squares regression; cell entries are OLS regression coefficients (standard errors are in parentheses).

*Excluded baseline income category is $50,000–$105,000.

Dependent variable: Egalitarianism (Individualism) factor score, rescaled from 0–100 to facilitate interpretation. **$p<0.05$; *$p<0.10$.

[‡] Models include controls for year of study not shown in the table.

Source: American National Election Studies, 1996, 2000, 2004, weighted data.

simply standing in as substitutes for affluence. The results in Table 6.2 show that homeownership is an especially strong and consistent predictor of individualistic attitudes and resistance to egalitarianism. Self-employment generally has a positive impact on individualism and a negative impact on egalitarianism, but is not always statistically significant.

Generally, however, rural residence does not play a significant role independent of the geographic distribution of self-employment and homeownership (see Table 6.2). If rural areas do stand apart from other locations in their propensity to favor individualism and express skepticism about egalitarian policies, it is primarily because there are more homeowners and self-employed workers in rural areas than there are in more urbanized areas. Place of residence alone is not a highly significant explanatory factor in this instance. However, the interaction of rural place of residence and homeownership lowers commitment to egalitarianism, and the interaction of rural place of residence and self-employment increases individualism.

Furthermore, commitment to egalitarianism and preference for individual rights and limited government are closely associated with—and perhaps determinative of—the direction and strength of party identification (see Figure 6.3). Religiously anchored moral views also play an important role, but these are not the only source of identification with the Republican Party.

FIGURE 6.3   INDIVIDUALISM AND EQUALITY BY DIRECTION AND STRENGTH
OF PARTY IDENTIFICATION

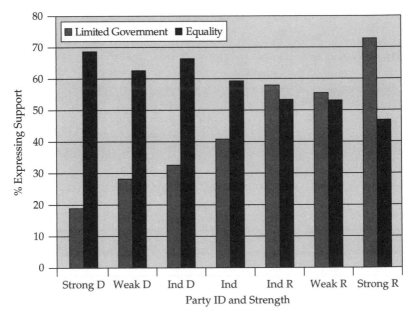

Source: American National Election Studies, 1996, 2000, 2004.

WEEDING OUT THE FAILURES: LABOR MARKET MIGRATION

Corporate America has extended its reach from farming into small-town banking, wholesale and retail trade, and, increasingly, service provision. True, corporate interests, such as agricultural intermediaries in meatpacking and food processing, are sometimes at odds with the interests of farmers and ranchers, but other rural Americans have come to depend on employment with these companies. Besides, government rarely has shown any willingness to regulate the consolidation and concentration of these industries, so there is little the small producer can do politically to effectuate change. They have learned that neither political party will respond to complaints, so they struggle on or find work elsewhere.

The economic consequences of globalization have been mixed. Large corporations are thought to be hostile to the interests of Main Street, as evidenced by the various battles Wal-Mart has faced when trying to locate stores in certain areas. But in almost every case, when a "big box" retail store moves in, one person's loss is someone else's gain. Many rural residents appreciate shopping in large-inventory stores full of a wide range of inexpensive merchandise. Consistent with their self-image as independent entrepreneurs, small retailers often will close their struggling enterprise, leaving town to find employment elsewhere. Population mobility allows labor market supply and demand to remain in equilibrium in rural America. The next time a pollster calls rural residents, a large share of those who have failed economically in the preceding decade may no longer be there to answer the telephone, while those who remain report that the local economy has remained about the same. Political discontent in reaction to economic downturn is difficult to gauge because different people constitute the rural electorate in every successive election.

The challenging task for the student of rural economic grievance is to locate *displaced* rural workers, who would be far more likely to express economic discontent. Economic decline in rural areas typically has been accompanied by steady population losses; this has been less true of metro areas facing the same extent of decline. Table 6.3 shows that net migration (population gain minus population loss due to mobility) between 1990 and 2000 dropped in rural locations as a consequence of rising unemployment in the previous decade and the base level of agricultural employment in 1990. Notably, it is the *change* in unemployment that drives migration out of rural areas, not the absolute level of unemployment (or income). Residents of many rural counties that have experienced sustained high unemployment rates over long periods have learned to live with a modicum of joblessness. Metropolitan locations, however, saw no corresponding drop in migration as a consequence of rising unemployment.

Because of the stigma associated with receiving public assistance, rural Americans who struggle economically and have no family to draw upon for support usually leave to seek work elsewhere, instead of accepting welfare benefits. This migration can be prohibitively costly, but White rural residents

TABLE 6.3   PREDICTORS OF NET MIGRATION BETWEEN 1990 AND 2000 IN U.S. COUNTIES, BY COUNTY SIZE

VARIABLE	NON-METRO <10,000	NON-METRO <25,000	METRO COUNTIES
Constant	−16.261** (4.984)	−19.547** (3.018)	−30.068** (3.343)
Increase in unemployment, 1980–1990	−0.443** (0.141)	−.393** (.088)	.113 (.117)
Median income, 1990 ($1,000s)	−0.008 (0.091)	.071 (.053)	.296** (.040)
Median age, 1990	0.622** (0.111)	.703** (.073)	.775** (.090)
Percent working in agriculture, 1990	−0.288** (0.048)	−.317** (.032)	.243** (.083)
Percent working in manufacturing, 1990	0.042 (0.054)	−.033 (.028)	−.104** (.029)
Population density, 1990 (1000s)	−3.377 (3.304)	−5.979** (1.759)	−.769** (.143)
Spatial lag of net migration in neighboring counties	0.389** (0.037)	.520** (.025)	.535** (.026)
N	665	1450	1666
-2 log likelihood	−2,565.05	−5,443.77	−6,415.22
P	0.0001	0.0001	0.0001
R^2	0.32	0.41	0.32

Spatially weighted regression; Maximum likelihood estimation; cell entries are regression coefficients (standard errors are in parentheses). Dependent variable: Percent growth or decline due to net migration between 1990 and 2000. **$p<0.05$.

Source: U.S. Census Bureau and Paul R. Voss, Scott McNiven, Roger B. Hammer, and Kenneth M. Johnson, County Specific Net Migration by Five-Year Age Groups, Hispanic, Origin, Race and Sex, 1990–2000 (Ann Arbor, Michigan: Inter-university Consortium for Political and Social Research, 2005).

usually will not meet with the kind of racial discrimination that traps African Americans in bad urban labor markets. So long as one has the means to pack up, travel, and afford a first and last month's rent payment at the destination, labor market migration can proceed with some efficiency. The massive twentieth-century outflow of labor surpluses from the rural South to northern cities and from the Midwest and southern plains to the nation's west coast are clear examples of the human capital generalization that people move from areas of poor opportunity to places where jobs can be found. Rural locations consistently have lower unemployment rates than big cities, not because the rural economy is always better, but because of the way in which rural workers respond to hard times.

CONCLUSION

Nearly every recent survey shows that rural Americans are more religiously and morally conservative than those living elsewhere. But this conservatism is not the only reason why rural Americans have been less inclined to vote for Democratic candidates in contemporary presidential elections. In spite of prevailing low income, their individualistic ethic and legacy of self-employment and homeownership inclines them to adopt the self-image of the independent entrepreneur and property owner rather than that of the laborer in need of state regulation and protection. Perhaps it is for this reason that rural allegiance to the Democratic Party during the New Deal era was temporary and fleeting.[24]

Rural Republican voters are not daft. Serious inquiry into a subject must not begin by taking a prejudicial posture toward it—even if the promulgation of common stereotypes makes the storyline easy to believe. To the extent that we can say that the electoral color of rural America is Republican red rather than Democratic blue, we can cite a variety of concrete explanations for this trend, some anchored in moral views and religious beliefs and others anchored in economic self-perception. The Republican Party's emphasis on personal effort, limited government, and free markets fits comfortably within the self-image of many rural Americans. There are always exceptions to these core commitments, but these are easily rationalized without abandoning basic principles.

Labor market out-migration has kept the supply and demand for labor in a respectable equilibrium, resulting in lower unemployment rates in small towns than in larger cities. Certainly, there are rural counties with high unemployment rates (Appalachian poverty springs readily to mind), but the scale of the problem is small relative to urban unemployment. Legions of Appalachian families have packed up and moved to Atlanta, Charlotte, Cincinnati, and other growing cities, leaving their hometowns smaller, but with less poverty and unemployment than would have been present otherwise. These moves usually result in substantial improvements in income for the displaced, although the rural poor sometimes become the urban poor. Those who remain in rural areas arguably suffer less than they would have if the surplus labor had remained in surplus. Rural industries now regularly resort to importing immigrants to fill jobs in food-processing industries that were once filled by the native-born.

Perhaps rural Americans report greater life satisfaction because steady out-migration in the face of globalization has made rural life sustainable at an acceptable, though far from luxurious, standard of living. Rural voters with economic grievances against government are fewer and farther between than is the case in cities and suburbs. Perhaps we now have the explanation Bartels[25] never provides for why working-class White voters position themselves *closer* to the Republican Party than they do to the Democrats on economic issues. The Democrats are not an attractive party for rural Americans, not only because of their positions on key socio-moral issues (including gay rights, abortion, and school prayer), but also because many rural Americans doubt whether typical Democratic *economic* positions fit with what they believe is true about themselves and the world.

NOTES

[1]See Matt Bai, "The Inside Agitator," *New York Times Magazine* (October 1, 2006): 54–60.

[2]But see Michael S. Lewis-Beck, "Agrarian Political Behavior in the United States," *American Journal of Political Science* 21 (1977): 543–565.

[3]These figures are based on the more expansive definition of "rural" as nonmetropolitan counties with populations smaller than 25,000. If we use the stricter definition of populations less than 10,000, the rural population is even *less Southern*, with 38 percent of voting age residents residing in Deep South and Border States.

[4]Edward C. Banfield and James Q. Wilson, *City Politics* (Cambridge, MA: Harvard University Press, 1963); Robert W. Kweit and Mary Grisez Kweit, *People and Politics in Urban America*, 2nd ed. (New York: Garland, 1999); William Julius Wilson, *The Truly Disadvantaged: The Inner City, the Underclass, and Public Policy* (Chicago: University of Chicago Press, 1987); William Julius Wilson, *When Work Disappears: The World of the New Urban Poor* (New York: Knopf, 1996).

[5]Wilson (1987, 1996).

[6]Joe R. Feagin and Harlan Hahn, *Ghetto Revolts: The Politics of Violence in American Cities* (New York: Macmillan, 1973).

[7]Robert Dahl, *Who Governs? Democracy and Power in an American City* (New Haven, CT: Yale University Press, 1961).

[8]Karen M. Kaufmann, *The Urban Voter: Group Conflict and Mayoral Voting Behavior in American Cities* (Ann Arbor: University of Michigan Press, 2004).

[9]V. O. Key, *Southern Politics in State and Nation* (New York: Vintage, 1949).

[10]Thomas Frank, *What's the Matter with Kansas: How Conservatives Won the Heart of America* (New York: Metropolitan Books, 2004).

[11]Michael S. Waters, *A Mathematics Educator's Introduction to Rural Policy Issues* (Athens, OH: Ohio University ACCLAIM Research Initiative, 2005).

[12]Jim Goad, *The Redneck Manifesto* (New York: Touchstone Books, 1997); Rebecca Thomas Kirkendall, "Who's a Hillbilly?" *Newsweek* (November 27, 1995): 22.

[13]Rob Moll, "Amish in the City: Has Reality TV Gone too Far?" *Christianity Today.com*, http://www.christianitytoday.com/ct/2004/103/31.0.html, accessed September 22, 2004.

[14]Lucy Jarosz and Victoria Lawson, "'Sophisticated People versus Rednecks': Economic Restructuring and Class Difference in America's West," *Antipode* 34 (2002): 13; see also Goad (1997).

[15]Larry Bartels, "What's the Matter with 'What's the Matter with Kansas'?" Paper presented at the annual meeting of the American Political Science Association, Washington, DC, September 1–4, 2005.

[16]Renee Drury and Luther Tweeten, "Have Farmers Lost Their Uniqueness?" *Review of Agricultural Economics* 19 (1997): 58–90; Oscar B. Martinson and E. A. Wilkening, "Rural-Urban Differences in Job Satisfaction: Further Evidence," *The Academy of Management Journal* 27

(1984): 199–206; Willard Rodgers, "Residential Satisfaction in Relationship to Size of Place," *Social Psychology Quarterly* 43 (1980): 436–441.

[17]Martinson and Wilkening (1984): 204.

[18]See, for example, Robert Putnam, *Bowling Alone: The Collapse and Revival of American Community* (New York: Simon and Schuster, 2000): chapter 20.

[19]Stanley Feldman, "Structure and Consistency in Public Opinion: The Role of Core Beliefs and Values," *American Journal of Political Science* 32 (1988): 416–440; Stanley Feldman and John Zaller, "The Political Culture of Ambivalence: Ideological Responses to the Welfare States," *American Journal of Political Science* 36 (1992): 268–307; David Knoke and Constance Henry, "Political Structure of Rural America," *Annals of the American Academy of Political and Social Science* 429 (1977): 51–62; Herbert McClosky and John Zaller, *The American Ethos* (Cambridge, MA: Harvard University Press, 1984).

[20]Edward S. Greenberg, "Industrial Self-Management and Political Attitudes," *American Political Science Review* 75 (1981): 29–42.

[21]Friedrich Engels, *The Housing Question* (Moscow: Progress Publishers, 1975); Greenberg (1981).

[22]Frederick H. Buttel and William L. Flinn, "Sources and Consequences of Agrarian Values in American Society," *Rural Sociology* 40 (1975): 134–151; William L. Flinn and Frederick H. Buttel, "Sociological Aspects of Farm Size: Ideological and Social Consequences of Scale in Agriculture," *American Journal of Agricultural Economics* 62 (1980): 946–953.

[23]Feldman (1988).

[24]James G. Gimpel and Jason E. Schuknecht, *Patchwork Nation: Sectionalism and Political Change in American Politics* (Ann Arbor: University of Michigan Press, 2003).

[25]Bartels (2005).

7

THE GENDER GAP*

❖

KAREN M. KAUFMANN

Both political party strategies and popular rhetoric surrounding presidential campaigns routinely emphasize the influence of gender on American voting behavior. This has been particularly true in recent presidential elections cycles, when Republican margins of victory in 2000 and 2004 were nothing less than razor thin. Accounts of "Soccer Moms," "Angry White Males," "NASCAR Dads," and "Security Moms" have peppered the airwaves and newspaper accounts of modern presidential campaigns, often suggesting that the Republican and Democratic Parties' electoral fortunes hinge on their respective abilities to attract male and female voters. Is this really the case?

Over the past 40 years, women have remained relatively loyal to the Democrats while men have moved solidly into the Republican column. In spite of this trend, the differences between men and women are still more like a ravine than a canyon. Partisan allegiances and voting choices between men and women do differ, but in recent years the gender gap has paled in comparison to racial and religious gaps in the American electorate. Nevertheless, in a competitive electoral environment, even small political differences in the voting preferences of men and women can decide elections. Thus, the gender gap continues to be of interest to scholars, political strategists, candidates, and pundits. Since women and men typically vote at comparable rates, the gender makeup of the electorate favors women (who comprise 52 percent of the U.S. population) over men. Gender differences in political choices are magnified by the unequal distribution of men and women in the electorate.

The first part of this chapter documents the contemporary history of the gender gap using trend data from the American National Election Studies (ANES). In particular, I focus on the sources of gender differences in American

*Previously published as K.M. Kaufmann, "The Gender Gap." *PS: Political Science and Politics* 39 (2006): 447–453. Reprinted with the permission of Cambridge University Press.

politics. The remainder of the chapter pays special attention to the most recent presidential elections, especially 2004, with an eye toward explaining the expansion and subsequent contraction of the gender gap in presidential voting. The chapter concludes with a discussion about the likely trajectory of the gender gap and its importance to the future of the American party system.

THE HISTORY OF THE MODERN GENDER GAP: 1952 TO 2004

The "gender gap" is traditionally understood to refer to the partisan difference between women and men.[1] There have long been gender differences in both party identification and vote choice, but the magnitude of the gender gap has been particularly prominent in the last two decades. As shown in Figure 7.1, women were approximately five percentage points more Republican than men during the 1950s. Beginning with the Johnson–Goldwater contest in 1964, however, women became more Democratic than men. With the exception of 1976 (when the gender gap virtually disappeared in the wake of the Watergate scandal, Nixon's resignation, and subsequent pardon), the political difference between women and men grew rather consistently up to and including 1996, when women were a full 14 percentage points more Democratic in their partisanship and voting behavior than men. Since then, the gender gap has declined somewhat; the 2004 gender gap in party identification shrank to 9.5 percentage

FIGURE 7.1 GENDER GAP IN PRESIDENTIAL VOTING AND PARTY IDENTIFICATION, 1952–2004

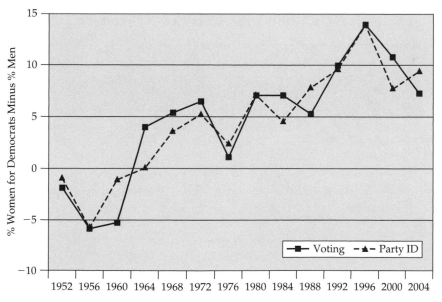

Source: American National Election Studies, 1952–2004.

points and the voting gap was only 7 percentage points. To put this in context, consider that the 2004 vote gap was only half of what it had been at its apex in 1996. While we should not make too much of one single point in time, a sustained contraction of the gender gap could pose rather dire circumstances for the Democratic Party, or, conversely, great fortune for the Republicans.

WHAT CAUSES THE GENDER GAP?

Although the gender gap has been an ongoing feature of American political behavior for a long time, scholarly interest in the gender gap began in earnest during the Reagan era. Early studies of the gender gap focused almost exclusively on women being the causal force behind growing gender divide in American politics.[2] In the wake of the women's movement of the 1970s, scholars disproportionately worked to understand the economic circumstances, group consciousness, and policy views of *women* to explain the growing political difference between women and men.[3] Contemporary analyses, however, clearly point to the changing politics of *men* as being the long-term, structural foundation of the gender gap.[4] From 1952 to 2004, the percentage of women identifying with the Republican Party declined by only five percentage points (moving from 58 percent to 53 percent). During this same period, male Democratic Party identification dropped from 59 percent to 43 percent: a difference of 16 percentage points (see Figure 7.2).

This pattern is even more pronounced among White voters. Figure 7.3 displays the percentage of White women and men identifying with the

FIGURE 7.2   DEMOCRATIC PARTY IDENTIFICATION BY GENDER, 1952–2004

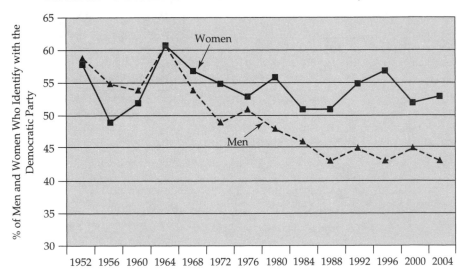

Source: American National Elections Studies, 1952–2004.

FIGURE 7.3   GENDER DIFFERENCES IN PARTY IDENTIFICATION AMONG WHITES,
1952–2004

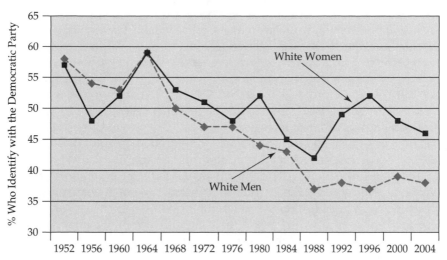

Source: American National Election Studies, 1952–2004.

Democratic Party in each presidential election year, beginning in 1952. Over this
time period, White women become nine percentage points less Democratic
(with their support dropping to 46 percent by 2004). On the other hand, White
men's support for the Democrats drops by a full 21 percentage points by 1988
(moving from 58 percent to 37 percent), at which point the trend flattens.

The pattern that is evident in Figure 7.3 clearly illustrates two distinct periods in the recent history of the gender gap. From the 1950s to the 1980s, men and
women were both becoming more Republican. However, it was the disproportionately large movement among men into the Republican Party that "created" the gender gap. Since the 1990s, male partisanship has remained
unmoved, while female partisanship is considerably more variable. Therefore,
recent changes in the gender gap must be attributable to fluctuations in the politics of women.[5] Political shifts among men may have created the gender gap,
but recent political variability among women is what causes it to persist.

GENDER DIFFERENCES IN POLITICAL ATTITUDES

Much of the research on the gender gap points to differences in the policy
views of men and women to explain broader gender differences in political
behavior. Men are more conservative than women across a number of important political domains, and these differences have behavioral implications.[6]

The most enduring attitudinal difference between men and women per-
tains to their views on whether the U.S. government ought to provide financial

assistance to the less fortunate. On questions regarding the proper role of government, desired levels of public services, as well as optimal levels of spending on social safety-net programs, women are typically five to eight percentage points more liberal than men.[7] On military matters, men are more hawkish than women, although the actual magnitude of gender differences on use-of-force issues varies somewhat from case to case.[8] The relative female distaste for military aggression remains evident in 2004, however, as women were more critical than men of the war in Iraq. According to the 2004 ANES, 62 percent of women report that the war was " not worth it" compared to 56 percent of men.

Surprisingly, gender differences are negligible on most of the hot-button social issues. Women and men are notably like-minded on questions of female equality, abortion rights, school prayer, and minority rights.[9] Attitudes regarding gay rights, however, have traditionally generated large differences between men and women. During the 1990s and early 2000s, women were much more supportive of gay rights than men—often by double-digit margins.[10] On the question of gay marriage, however, female liberalism wanes; men and women hold nearly identical views on this specific question.

While considerable evidence suggests that public opinion on a wide range of issues may ebb and flow over the years, differences between the political views of men are women are actually quite stable over time. The data in Figure 7.4 represent the average female and male responses to identical questions asked in

FIGURE 7.4   THE DIFFERENCE BETWEEN MALE AND FEMALE ATTITUDES, 1988 TO 2004

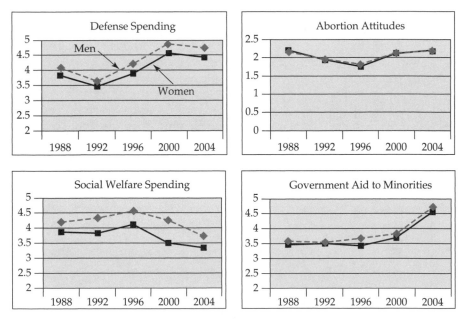

Source: American National Election Studies, 1988–2004.

the past five ANES surveys regarding attitudes toward four key issues: defense, social welfare, abortion, and government aid to minorities. Higher values represent more conservative responses. The graphs indicate that even when overall mean values rise and fall, the differences between men's and women's attitudes remain largely unchanged. Put simply, men and women have *not* become more polarized over political issues during the past 16 years. Therefore, changes in the gender gap during this period are most likely a result of changes in the *relative importance* men and women place on various issues of the day.

WHAT WOMEN AND MEN REALLY CARE ABOUT

To the extent that differences in the political views of men and women have remained relatively constant over the past 16 years, it is fairly safe to assume that changes in the size of the gender gap result from the fact that men and women place different emphasis on certain political issues when they formulate their party identification and vote choices. The gender gap grew considerably during the Clinton era, and research suggests that female resurgence to the Democratic Party during the 1990s was fueled by the relatively greater importance that women placed on social issues.[11] Questions of social equality (specifically, women's rights and gay rights) increasingly informed women's partisan orientations during the Clinton era, but did not have a similar direct effect on the partisanship of men.[12] It appears that the "culture wars" that waged during the 1990s[13] made social issues feel particularly salient to women and therefore resulted in the large gender gap in voting during this period. Similar analyses conducted for the period from 1996 to 2004 show that attitudes on socio-moral issues have continued to influence the partisan choices of women more than is the case for men. At the same time, the influence of women's views on such issues on their party identification has remained quite stable since 1996. Gender differences regarding the importance of social equality therefore cannot explain the recent contraction of the gender gap, especially in 2004.

THE GENDER GAP IN 2004

As shown in Figures 7.2 and 7.3, the Democratic Party was particularly attractive to women during the Bill Clinton era. By 2004, however, female enthusiasm for the Democratic Party and its presidential nominee had waned. Especially noteworthy is the fact that in 2004, the gender gap in voting reached a 12-year low. One possible explanation for the narrowing of the gender gap is that male–female differences in policy views may have been smaller in 2004 than in prior years. However, recall that Figure 7.4 provides evidence that gender differences in issue opinions vary little over time. Men and women have *not* become more or less polarized on many traditional political issues over recent election cycles.

Given the increased prominence of national security issues since the September 11, 2001 terrorist attacks and the beginning of the war in Iraq, voting in 2004 might reflect uncharacteristic unity between the genders. If men and women equally support or oppose the war effort, we would be likely to see a reduction in the overall gender gap. The data in Figure 7.5, however, suggest otherwise. On three key questions—George W. Bush's handling of the war in Iraq, whether the war was "worth it," and whether the United States is now more or less secure—consistent male–female differences emerge. As has been the case historically, men are considerably more hawkish than women across all three measures.

Public opinion data from 2004 indicate that male–female differences in political views are largely consistent with prior years. Men are more conservative on social welfare issues, more hawkish on war-related concerns, and quite comparable to women on attitudes toward abortion, female equality, and gay marriage. Thus, recent changes in public opinion would not appear to explain the diminishing size of the gender divide. If the gender gap in *views* on issues did not change in 2004, then perhaps changes in issue *priorities* can explain the waning divide.

FIGURE 7.5   NATIONAL SECURITY AND WAR OPINIONS BY GENDER

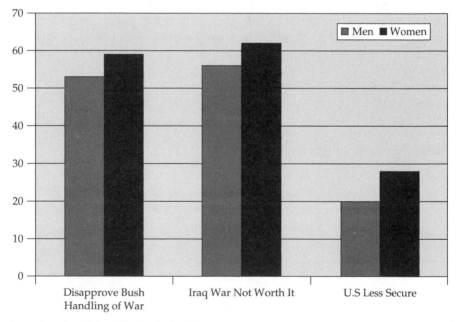

Source: American National Election Study, 2004.

In order to explore this possibility, I created a statistical model of the 2004 vote by gender. The results of this analysis are found in Table 7.1. I explain the vote for President Bush using party identification, income, education, age, race, as well as opinions on a range of policies atop the 2004 public agenda. The War/National Security measure combines opinions on Bush's handling of the war, whether the war was worth it, and whether the Bush administration has made the United States more or less secure. The National Economy variable is an evaluation of the U.S. economy over the past four years. The Personal Finances measure is an appraisal of whether one's personal finances have improved or worsened over the past year. The Abortion and Gay Marriage variables gauge support or opposition to legal abortion and gay marriage. The Social Welfare Attitudes variable combines three questions pertaining to the appropriate size of government and its responsibility to provide health care and jobs.[14]

Table 7.1 confirms the conventional wisdom that opinions regarding the war and national security were particularly consequential to the 2004 vote. Even controlling for the traditionally powerful effects of partisanship, war and national security concerns meaningfully shape voting behavior for both men and women. Also noteworthy is the fact that there are no significant differences between men and women with respect to party identification and war

TABLE 7.1   THE 2004 PRESIDENTIAL VOTE AMONG MEN AND WOMEN

	MEN			WOMEN		
	B	S.E.	SIG.	B	S.E.	SIG.
Party Identification	6.61	(1.06)	0.000	5.28	(0.83)	0.000
War/National Security	4.99	(1.30)	0.000	4.64	(1.28)	0.000
National Economy	2.70	(1.04)	0.010	1.97	(1.20)	0.101
Personal Finances	0.28	(0.62)	0.648	0.36	(0.58)	0.411
Abortion	1.45	(0.83)	0.080	−0.31	(0.77)	0.691
Same-sex Marriage	1.03	(0.59)	0.084	1.32	(0.57)	0.022
Social Welfare	1.95	(1.08)	0.624	2.03	(1.15)	0.077
Constant	−4.99	(1.64)	.002	−2.75	(1.79)	0.123
% Correctly predicted	0.91			0.91		
N	295			301		

Note: Cell entries are logistic regression coefficients with standard errors in parentheses. The dependent variable is presidential vote (Bush=1, else=0). All independent variables are scaled from zero to one. Controls for age, income, education, and race are included in the model, but not shown.

Source: American National Election Study, 2004.

attitudes. Put simply, there were no large discrepancies in issue salience between men and women in 2004. This means that men and women used a similar calculus in making their vote decisions, so the results of my analysis do not support the proposition that the contraction of the gender gap can be traced to important differences in the issues that matter most to men and women.

WAS IT THE SECURITY MOMS?

One of the more popular media accounts coming out of the 2004 election suggested that the "soccer moms" of the 1990s had turned into "security moms."[15] Once considered an important swing constituency for the Democrats, these anxious mothers were now said to be swinging to the Republicans over issues of national security. Always looking for nifty storytelling aids, the media seized on the myth of the security mom, and it instantly became conventional wisdom. The only problem is that the myth was not true.[16]

The 2004 ANES data show that mothers with children at home were no more likely to vote for Bush in 2004 than they had been in 2000. As shown in Figure 7.6, approximately 50 percent of women with children at home voted for Bush in 2000, while 49 percent voted for him in 2004. If anything, the Republicans appear to have picked up votes among women without children at home: 44 percent of them supported him in 2000 versus 51 percent in 2004. Additionally, the ANES data reveal that mothers were no more likely to worry about national security than were women without children at home.

FIGURE 7.6   THE SECURITY MOM MYTH

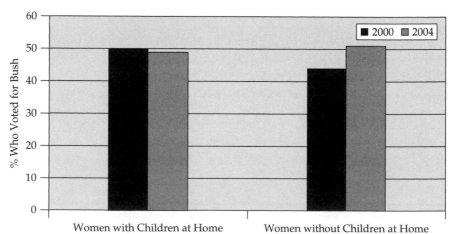

Source: American National Election Studies, 2000 and 2004.

The most important gender-related story from the 2004 election had little to do with the mythical security mom; rather, regional differences in the gender gap between White men and women appear to explain why the overall gap between men and women was so much smaller at the ballot box in 2004. *Southern* White women moved to the Republican Party and supported George W. Bush in much higher proportions than had been the case in the recent past. Although the gender gap between White southern men and women was a full 11 percentage points in 2000, it fell to only 5 points in 2004. Even more striking is the fact that the presidential vote gap in the South hit its lowest point in 40 years in 2004 (see Figure 7.7). Compared to White southern men, White southern women chose Bill Clinton over Bob Dole by a 17-point margin in 1996 and preferred Al Gore to George W. Bush by 9 percentage points in 2000. In 2004, however, southern women favored *Bush* by a two-point margin *over* southern men.[17] Yet the collapse of the southern gender gap was not mirrored in other regions of the United States. Outside of the South, the male–female divide in the vote actually increased slightly from a nine-point difference in 2000 to a ten-point difference in 2004.

The 2004 election was notable for its high level of partisan voting. Relatively few voters crossed party lines. However, southern women were conspicuous exceptions to this rule. Among self-identified White Democrats, 88 percent of southern men, 90 percent of non-southern men, 91 percent of non-southern

FIGURE 7.7   WHITE GENDER GAP IN PRESIDENTIAL VOTING: SOUTH VS. NON-SOUTH

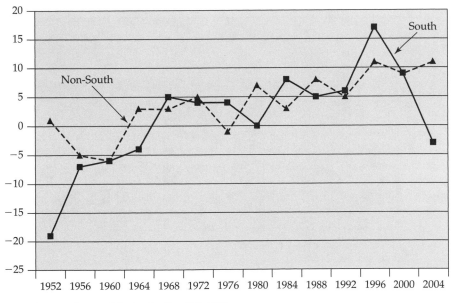

Source: American National Election Studies, 1952–2004.

women, but only 75 percent of southern women cast their votes for John Kerry. Conversely, southern women were the most loyal Republican partisans, with 98 percent voting for Bush.

Of the many reasons that southern women may disproportionately have preferred Bush in 2004, the most obvious potential explanation surrounds questions of war and national security. These issues were specific to the 2004 election, and had an extremely significant effect on voting behavior (as evidenced in Table 7.1). If southern women were more supportive of the war in Iraq than were non-southern women, we might have an explanation for the high Democratic Party defection rates as well as the collapse of the vote gap in the South.

The data in Figure 7.8 reveal gender and regional differences in attitudes toward national security concerns and opinion about the war in Iraq among White voters. While the size of the gender gap on the question of Bush's handling of the war is roughly equal in the South and elsewhere (a six-point gap in the South versus an eight-point gap elsewhere), the southern gender gaps on whether the war was worth it and whether the administration had made the United States more or less secure were only two points and one point, respectively. Gender discrepancies outside of the South were considerably larger: eight points on whether the war was worth it and eleven points on the question of national security. The regional differences between southern and non-southern women are greater than male–female differences. Southern women are 19 points more approving of Bush's handling of the war than are

FIGURE 7.8   WHITE OPINION ON WAR ISSUES: GENDER AND REGIONAL DIFFERENCES

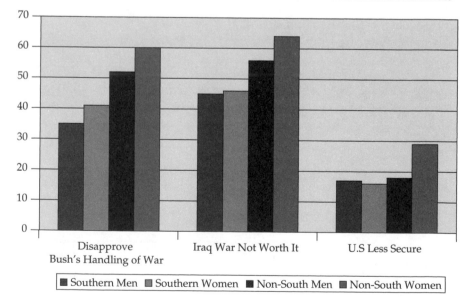

Source: American National Election Study, 2004.

women elsewhere; they are 18 points more likely to say that the war has been worth it; and they are 13 points less critical of the administration on the national security issue. In all, White southerners (both men and women) supported the war effort to a much greater degree than did people living outside of the South. The combination of smaller gender differences in the South and the particularly high level of importance that all voters assigned to war-related issues in 2004 combine to help explain the shrinking gender gap.

Finally, this research points to significant differences in the way in which women in the South and women elsewhere evaluate political candidates. The ANES asks respondents to rate the major party candidates on a variety of traits such as morality, leadership skills, and whether the candidate "really cares about people like you." The standard trait question poses a statement (such as "[Candidate's name] is moral") and asks the respondent how well the statement describes the candidate. Possible answers are arrayed on a four-point scale from "extremely well" to "not well at all." In general, individual perceptions of candidate traits often are imbued with substantial partisan overtones. Republicans tend to evaluate Republican candidates more positively, just as Democrats tend to think better of Democratic candidates, but divergent opinions regarding Bush and Kerry extended well beyond the partisan divide.

Figure 7.9 presents the difference in average trait evaluations between southern and non-southern women for George W. Bush and John Kerry. Across the

FIGURE 7.9   MEAN DIFFERENCES IN TRAIT EVALUATIONS (1–4 SCALE) BETWEEN SOUTHERN AND NON-SOUTHERN WOMEN: BUSH VS. KERRY

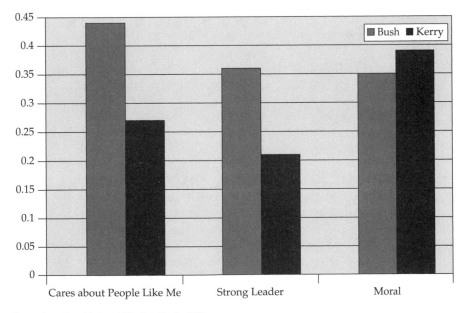

Source: American National Election Study; 2004.

three traits mentioned, regional differences in the mean scores are substantial and statistically significant. The regional disparities between trait ratings of Bush are (on average) more substantial than differences in southern and non-southern opinions of Kerry. The largest discrepancy between the women in the South and non-South appears on the question of whether Bush "cares about people like you." In this instance, it is quite clear that southern women feel a greater personal connection to Bush than do women who live outside of the South.

Regional discrepancies in women's ratings of Bush are also much greater in 2004 than was the case four years earlier. The mean difference in ratings of Bush between southern women and non-southern women in 2000 and in 2004 is displayed in Figure 7.10. On the questions of caring and morality, regional differences were statistically insignificant in 2000. The disparity regarding perceived leadership skill was about half as large in 2000 as it was in 2004. Bush was largely unknown to the mass public when he ran for office in 2000, and female perceptions of Bush's traits were not polarized by region. Over the course of the first Bush administration, however, southern women came to hold profoundly different views of the incumbent from those of their non-southern counterparts.[18]

Finally, it appears that the evaluation of candidates' personal traits matter more to the vote choice of southern women than they do to the vote choice of non-southern women. Figure 7.11 shows the partial correlations of Bush trait evaluations with presidential vote choice, controlling for party identification. The partial correlation is useful because it allows us to see how much trait evaluations

FIGURE 7.10   MEAN DIFFERENCES IN BUSH TRAIT SCORES (1–4 SCALE) BETWEEN SOUTHERN AND NON-SOUTHERN WOMEN: 2000 VS. 2004

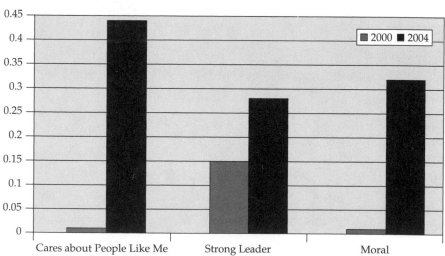

Source: American National Election Studies, 2000 and 2004.

FIGURE 7.11   PARTIAL CORRELATION WITH PRESIDENTIAL VOTE CONTROLLING
                    FOR PARTY ID—BUSH TRAITS

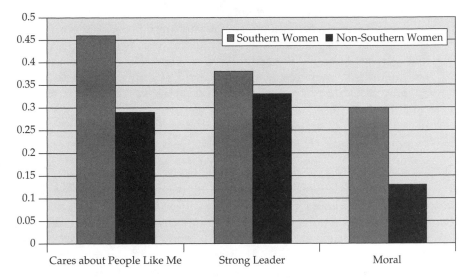

Source: American National Election Studies, 2004.

matter to vote choices above and beyond the effects of party identification. To the
extent that trait evaluations are party-colored opinions, they should exert little
independent influence over presidential vote choice. Figure 7.11, however,
clearly shows that this is not the case. Instead, candidate choice among White
southern women in 2004 was much more closely tied to perceived traits than
was candidate choice among non-southern women. This is especially true with
respect to perceptions of "caring." Southern Democratic women who felt that
Bush cared about people like them were more likely to defect from their partisan ties than were non-southern women with comparable views. What this
shows us is that political decisions are certainly not constrained to issue considerations. Candidate qualities often combine with policy views to attract or
repel voters. In the case of southern women, character traits appear to have
been particularly influential.

Additional analyses (not shown here) suggest that trait evaluations in general were more important to voting behavior in 2004 than they had been in
2000, particularly among southern women. It is not necessarily surprising that
candidate traits matter more when incumbents run for office. After all, retro-
spective evaluations of many sorts come into play during reelection campaigns
because voters have had the chance to develop a clear impression of the incumbent while he or she has been in office. By the same token, there is no good, the-
oretically grounded reason why southern women should be especially reliant
on candidate traits when they make their choices in the voting booth. In fact,

the pattern in 2004 deviates considerably from the previous presidential election with an incumbent on the ballot, 1996. In that election, regional trait differences were not nearly as pronounced. It is beyond the scope of this chapter to fully explain the unique regional patterns from 2004 (for more on this subject, see Chapter 6 in this volume). It seems worth noting, however, that Clinton, Gore, and Bush are all southerners of one stripe or another, and that the lukewarm response to John Kerry, especially among southern women, may reflect a preference among southerners for candidates who share their southern roots.

CONCLUSION

The gender gap in partisanship and voting behavior was notably modest in 2004, especially in comparison to its apex eight years earlier. The shrinking gender gap was not a universal phenomenon, however. Important regional differences in candidate trait evaluations and support for the war in Iraq appear to have mitigated the gender divide among White voters in the South. Historically, the southern gender gap has equaled or exceeded male–female political differences in other regions of the United States, but this was certainly not the case in 2004.

In hindsight we may find that the unique circumstances surrounding the 2004 election (since it was held in the aftermath of an unprecedented terrorist attack and in the midst of a U.S.-led military invasion) render this election an outlier. The gender gap traditionally is understood to be a function of male–female differences in public opinion and issue priorities. Therefore, to the extent that the importance of military concerns wanes over time in favor of more traditional domestic issues such as social welfare spending, the gender gap in the South may very well rise again. It is also possible that southern gender solidarity over military issues may waver.

It is important to remember that the war in Iraq was in its incipient stages during the 2004 presidential contest. War opinions were informed by partisanship to a much greater degree in 2004 than was the case in 2006 (during the writing of this chapter). It is certainly plausible that as partisan loyalty on the issue of the war gives way to other considerations, a gender gap regarding this matter may emerge in the South, as it already has elsewhere.

From the standpoint of the Democratic Party, the collapse of the southern gender gap may not be all that alarming. The Deep South states with the smallest gender differences have not been traditionally Democratic terrain for many years. Dynamic movement in the gender gap is most consequential when changes occur on contested terrain. It is in these "purple" states where the stakes of gender politics are particularly high. The analysis of the 2004 election suggests that the gender gap is alive and well outside of the South.

Nonetheless, the parties may need to think strategically about future candidates and future issue agendas if they wish to retain their respective gender advantages at the ballot box.

NOTES

[1]While there are many ways to measure the gender gap, the simplest and most widely used measure is the arithmetic difference between female and male preferences for the Democratic Party and the Democratic presidential candidate. The gender gaps in party identification illustrated in Figure 7.1 uses the standard seven-point party identification scale. Partisans include strong, weak, and leaning identifiers.

[2]But see Daniel Wirls, "Reinterpreting the Gender Gap,"*Public Opinion Quarterly* 50 (1986): 316–330.

[3]Steven P. Erie and Martin Rein, "Women and the Welfare State," in *The Politics of the Gender Gap: The Social Construction of Political Influence*, ed. Carol M. Mueller (Newbury Park, CA: Sage, 1988); Kathleen Frankovic, "Sex and Politics: New Alignments, Old Issues," *PS: Political Science and Politics* 15 (1982): 439–448; Frances Fox Piven, "Women and the State: Ideology, Power, and the Welfare State," in *Gender and the Life Course*, ed. Alice S. Rossi (New York: Aldine, 1985); Robert Y. Shapiro and Harpreet Mahajan, "Gender Differences in Policy Preferences: A Summary of Trends from the 1960s and 1980s," *Public Opinion Quarterly* 50 (1986): 42–61; Eleanor Smeal, *Why and How Women Will Elect the Next President* (New York: Harper and Row, 1984).

[4]Janet M. Box-Steffensmeier, Suzanna DeBoef, and Tse-Min Lin, "The Dynamics of the Partisan Gender Gap," *American Political Science Review* 98 (2004): 515–525; Carole K. Chaney, R. Michael Alvarez, and Jonathan Nagler, "Explaining the Gender Gap in the U.S. Presidential Elections, 1980–1992," *Political Research Quarterly* 51 (1998): 311–340; Karen M. Kaufmann and John R. Petrocik, "The Changing Politics of American Men: Understanding the Sources of the Gender Gap," *American Journal of Political Science* 43 (1999): 864–887; Barbara Norrander, "The Evolution of the Gender Gap," *Public Opinion Quarterly* 63 (1999): 566–576.

[5]Box-Steffensmeier, De Boef, and Lin (2004); Karen M. Kaufmann, "Culture Wars, Secular Realignment and the Gender Gap in Party Identification," *Political Behavior* 24 (2002): 283–307.

[6]Chaney, Alvarez, and Nagler (1998); Shapiro and Majahan (1986).

[7]Chaney, Alvarez, and Nagler (1998); Kaufmann and Petrocik (1999); Mark Schlesinger and Caroline Heldman, "Gender Gap or Gender Gaps? New Perspectives on Support for Government Action and Policies," *Journal of Politics* 63 (2001): 59–92; Shapiro and Mahajan (1986).

[8]Pamela Johnston Conover and Virginia Sapiro, "Gender, Feminist Consciousness, and War," *American Journal of Political Science* 37 (1993): 1079–1099; Robert S. Erikson and Kent L. Tedin, *American Public Opinion* (New York: Pearson Longman, 2005); Miroslav Nincic and Donna J. Nincic, "Race, Gender, and War," *Journal of Peace Research* 39 (2002): 547–568.

[9]Chaney, Alvarez, and Nagler (1998); Kaufmann and Petrocik (1999).

[10]Kaufmann (2002); Clyde Wilcox and Barbara Norrander, "Of Moods and Morals: The Dynamics of Opinion on Abortion and Gay Rights," in *Understanding Public Opinion*, 2nd ed., eds. Barbara Norrander and Clyde Wilcox (Washington, DC: CQ Press, 2002).

[11]Kaufmann (2002).

[12]Ibid.

[13]James Davison Hunter, *Culture Wars: The Struggle to Define America* (New York: Basic Books, 1991).

[14]All of these measures are scaled from zero to one to facilitate comparisons within and between models.

[15]See, for example, Mike Allen, "Bush Makes Pitch to 'Security Moms'," *Washington Post* (September 18, 2004): A14; Linda Feldman, "Why Women Are Edging toward Bush," *Christian Science Monitor* (September 23, 2004): 1.

[16]In the last weeks before the General Election, the media also began to discover that the "security mom" myth did not represent reality. See Richard Morin and Dan Balz, "'Security Mom' Bloc Proves Hard to Find," *Washington Post* (October 1, 2004): A5.

[17]Given the relatively small sample size of the 2004 ANES, I looked to verify this pattern using additional data. My analysis (not shown) using state exit poll data collected by Edison Media Research and Mitofsky International reveals similar patterns to the results using the ANES data. Furthermore, the gender gap in the South is not constant across southern *states*. There is considerable variance in the size of the gender gap across the 11 southern states, ranging from an eight-point margin in favor of the Democrats in Virginia, to a seven-point margin in favor of the Republicans in Mississippi. The gender gap in the remaining states fluctuates in a +/- three-point range around zero.

[18]The regional differences in candidate evaluations were not constant across genders, but they were particularly pronounced among women. Comparable analyses on the mean differences for men reveal smaller variations between the South and elsewhere.

8

THE GENERATION GAP

❖

ANAND EDWARD SOKHEY
PAUL A. DJUPE

Recent studies of electoral behavior have tended to put the variable of age on the sidelines, focusing instead on the effects of factors such as ideology, worship attendance, and political sophistication. Unfortunately, this trend has had the effect of reducing age to a sort of theoretical afterthought in studies of voting behavior.

Age deserves much more attention from scholars because to a certain degree it represents fundamental differences in the ways that citizens react to politics. Age-related distinctions, or put another way, generational differences, create "gaps" in the vote for certain candidates as well as divisions in political participation, political engagement, party identification, and public opinion. For example, political scientist Robert Putnam notes that older Americans belong to more organizations, vote more frequently, and read newspapers more often than younger Americans,[1] a finding frequently reported by other scholars.[2] Thus, age is more than just a control variable and more than just a way of expressing contemporary electoral divisions. Instead, it implies different *processes* of political socialization and experience. These processes give rise to the currently observable differences in political behavior and public opinion among the different generations active in American politics today.

AGE GROUPS, SOCIALIZATION, AND THE STUDY OF GENERATIONS

In thinking about how scholars study age and politics, a good place to start is with conventional political wisdom. One frequent assumption is that people become more conservative as they get older. On its face this seems like a reasonable inference (and there is actually some evidence to support this notion, as we will discuss below) since people earn and own more as they age. Older people are surely more risk-averse in general than they were in their teenage years. On the other hand, the assumption that older people are more conservative stands at odds with how we frequently talk about how (for instance) incoming college students arrive at their political views. It is common to note (flippantly), "that person just adopted their parents' voting habits." But if individuals acquire their political attachments and ideologies solely from their parents, we would expect *no* generational differences, because new voters would be just as Republican and/or conservative (or Democratic and/or liberal) as older voters. Reality, of course, is much different and more complex. Quite a few factors combine to explain both how people acquire their political attachments and orientations and whether (and how) these things change over time.

Although the study of age and politics has in some ways fallen out of favor within political science, at one time the examination of socialization and generational change was a fertile area among scholars of electoral politics. Researchers looked at how political attitudes and orientations toward the political world were formed during early childhood[3] and adolescence,[4] and they noted the roles of parents[5] and peers[6] in the transmission of political attitudes and party identification.

In the study of adult political socialization, scholars have focused primarily on the importance of *early* adulthood for shaping long-lasting political beliefs and behaviors. For years it has been assumed that the years from late adolescence into early adulthood (roughly between the ages of 17 and 26, although there is no agreement on the exact span[7]) are particularly impressionable ones, and that political attachments and views formed during this time are more likely to be long-lasting. From this focus came the study of *generational effects*, the idea that people who come of age in the same era differ politically from other generations for the remainder of their lives. For instance, for many decades political scientists spoke of the distinctive political attachments of the "New Deal Coalition," a diverse group of people whose experiences during the Great Depression gave rise to lifelong Democratic voting habits.

But people do pay attention to current events. They are affected by government actions, and they sometimes experience dramatic changes in their own lives once they pass through early adulthood. Should we not expect these experiences to encourage political change as well? From this perspective, generations have been examined in relation to two other types of adult socialization effects: *life cycle effects*, or changes that happen in individuals as they grow older (for example, rising health care costs or homeownership), and *period effects*, which are changes that occur in response to shared major life experiences that can cut across age groups.[8] Examples of such shared experiences would include the Great Depression, the World Wars, the 1970s oil crisis, and the terrorist attacks of September 11, 2001.

Much of the work on generational, life cycle, and period effects has examined changes in people's party identification and political ideology. Loosely based on these ideas, much of this research has been conducted in the context of "realignment theory." Now viewed less favorably by scholars, realignment theory was (and to a certain extent still is) a popular way of thinking about historical patterns in American electoral politics.[9] Political scientist V. O. Key first articulated a "critical theory of elections" as a way to argue that citizens can and do bring about major changes via the electoral process, which is an essential element of a legitimate democracy.[10] With later development by Walter Dean Burnham and James Sundquist, realignment theory aimed to explain eras when one political party seemed to dominate the other by examining the changing electoral bases of the parties. These scholars argued that such changes were rooted, in part, in a generational theory of political change.[11]

There is little evidence to suggest that individuals become more Republican as they get older,[12] but there is some support for lasting generational differences in party identification. Political scientists Robert Erikson and Kent Tedin note that people in their "impressionable years" during the Great Depression remained more Democratic than any other age group as recently as 1990. On the other hand, people who came of age during the 1920s (a time when the Republican Party was dominant) remained the most Republican age cohort in 1990.[13] Scholars also have found some support for life cycle effects in strength of partisanship and ideology, and for period effects in partisanship. Younger voters have weaker partisan attachments than older voters;[14] individuals become more conservative as they age;[15] and in the short run, each generation constantly shifts its partisanship by small amounts in response to current events.[16]

We can see some of these forces at work when we examine the degree to which a generational cohort maintains the same party identification over time. To illustrate this, we picked two famous generations to examine: (1) the "Greatest" Generation[17]: those born between 1911 and 1924 who were young adults at the time of World War II, and (2) the "Baby Boom" Generation: the huge cohort of Americans born in the aftermath of World War II (1945–1962). Using survey snapshots taken during presidential election years, the party affiliations of these generational cohorts are traced in Figure 8.1 from the start of their adult political lives until the present day.

The results suggest that these (and by inference, many) generations are politically distinctive. The oldest members of the Greatest Generation joined the electorate right at the onset of the Great Depression. They are roughly 10 percent more Democratic than their children, the Baby Boomers. Almost 50 percent of the Greatest Generation has been Democratic identifiers throughout their lives, while just 30 percent of Boomers have affiliated with the Democratic party up until their retirement years.

FIGURE 8.1   PERCENT DEMOCRATIC AFFILIATION AMONG THE GREATEST AND BABY
BOOM GENERATIONS

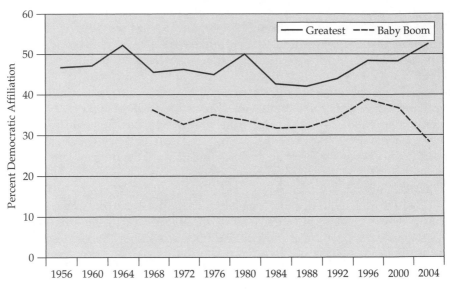

Source: NES Cumulative File, 1956–2004.

The evidence for period and life cycle effects, however, is less clear in Figure 8.1. There is some fluctuation from election year to election year. Greatest Generation members show a Democratic spike in 1964 (a landslide year overall for Lyndon Johnson) and a smaller spike for Jimmy Carter in 1980, just before reaching their lowest point of support for the Democratic Party in 1988. There is less movement in Boomer party affiliation, save the sharp dip after 1996 (which was the high point of their support for the Democrats). Until 1988, the trend in Greatest Generation Democratic support erodes steadily, although it encounters a few bumps along the way. After 1988, however, it climbs steadily until it matches 1964 levels. Perhaps not coincidentally, Greatest Generation support for the Democratic Party climbed just as most of the cohort reached retirement age in the 1980s. Since Democrats traditionally are viewed as more supportive of Social Security and Medicare, does this trend reflect the specific policy concerns of senior citizens? Should we consider this increase in support for the Democrats to be a life cycle effect (in response to changing *personal* circumstances) or a period effect? Surely to some extent it is a confluence of both effects, which highlights the difficulty of understanding just how age affects politics and politics affects age.

The implications of this pattern in support for the Democratic Party are also quite significant for the Baby Boom Generation. Since this large generation is just entering the retirement years, should we expect their political orientations to change? Will their support of the Democratic Party climb steadily as was the case with their parents? How will the parties respond to the potentially changing demands of this electoral powerhouse? The answers are by no means clear.

One way to assess the political significance of the demands of a given age group (such as the Baby Boom Generation) is to measure the relative size of different age groups in the electorate. The larger an age group's size in the electorate, the more incentive politicians will have to pay attention to the group's demands. Figure 8.2 examines the size of distinct generations in the electorate from 1956 to 2004; that is, in each presidential election survey, it shows the proportion of voters that were 18–24, 25–44, 45–64, and 65+. Although defining what constitutes a generation is a somewhat slippery matter, we choose these particular age cohorts because they are commonly used in research of this sort, and because they group respondents (roughly) according to shared life experiences.

One of the more obvious features demonstrated in Figure 8.2 is the jump in the proportion of the young (18–24) in the electorate in 1972. This increase was the result of the lowering of the voting age to 18 with the ratification of the Twenty-Sixth Amendment to the Constitution in 1971. It is also readily apparent that the American electorate is, overall, an aging one, with the proportion of voters aged 25–44 decreasing in the 1990s; the proportion of voters 45–64 increasing steadily as the Baby Boom Generation moves toward retirement; and the proportion of voters over 65 decreasing as the Greatest Generation passes on. Undoubtedly the demands of the 45- to 64-year-old generation (late-middle-aged citizens and younger seniors) are not lost on political candidates and elected officials.

FIGURE 8.2   AGE COMPOSITION OF THE AMERICAN ELECTORATE, 1956–2004

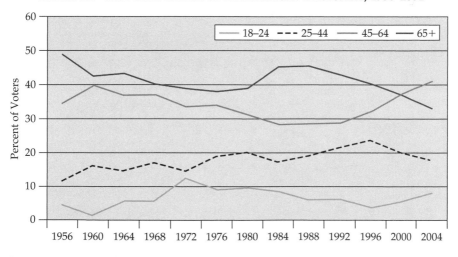

Source: NES Cumulative File, 1956–2004.

THE GENERATION GAP IN THE PRESIDENTIAL VOTE

As a prelude to examining the generation gap in the 2004 presidential election, we present the historical context of age differences in the presidential vote. Figure 8.3 shows the Democratic vote over the last thirteen presidential elections for the same four age groups examined in Figure 8.2.[18] The trend lines demonstrate how the electorate tends to move together. The electorate on the whole was dramatically Democratic in 1964 (electing Lyndon Johnson in a historic landslide) but far less so just eight years later (reelecting Richard Nixon for a second term in office). In some elections the electorate is not divided by age, instead tracking closely together (as in the election and reelection of Ronald Reagan), but at other times generational gaps appear. For instance, in the 1950s and 1960s, Americans over the age of 65 were among the most Republican voters, and their vote for Johnson in 1964 was highly restrained compared to the other groups. Likewise, young voters (ages 18–24) did not move toward Nixon in 1972, in part due to Democratic candidate George McGovern's concerted effort to capture their votes. Moreover, starting with Bill Clinton's first election in 1992 (with the exception of 1996), young voters have been much more Democratic than their elders. Interestingly, during this same time span, voters aged 65 and older have not consistently been among the most Republican cohorts in the electorate; in fact, they were the second most Democratic group in 2000.

Figure 8.4 illustrates these generational differences more clearly by detailing the difference in the Democratic presidential vote between (1) voters over and under the age of 40 and (2) voters aged 18–24 and their parents, aged 45–64. Each bar shows whether younger voters are more Democratic

FIGURE 8.3   DEMOCRATIC PRESIDENTIAL VOTE FOR AGE GROUPS, 1956–2004

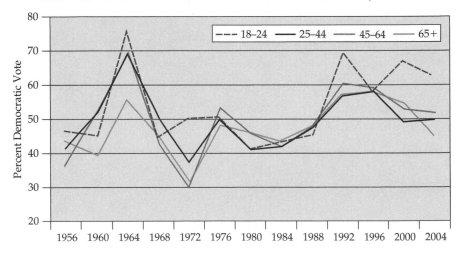

Source: NES Cumulative File, 1956–2004.

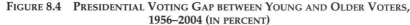

FIGURE 8.4   PRESIDENTIAL VOTING GAP BETWEEN YOUNG AND OLDER VOTERS,
1956–2004 (IN PERCENT)

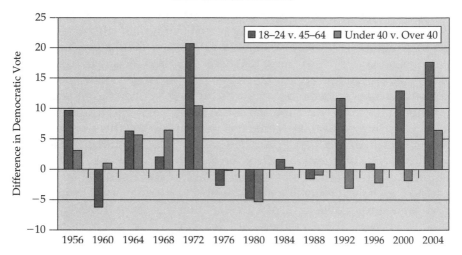

Source: NES Cumulative File, 1956–2004.

(a positive number) or less Democratic (a negative number) than their elders. Over this time period younger people are clearly more Democratic, although the intergenerational differences are not overwhelmingly large. In about three-quarters of recent presidential elections, the vote choice gap is no larger than five percentage points. In a few cases, however, this gap is substantial. Younger voters preferred Adlai Stevenson in 1956, Johnson in 1964, McGovern in 1972, Clinton in 1992, Al Gore in 2000, and John Kerry in 2004 by much greater margins than did their elders. In several cases young people were more Republican than their elders, for example preferring Nixon in 1960 and Reagan in 1980, but the differences are not as substantial.

Figure 8.4 also assists us by demonstrating that the specific way in which the age gap is measured partially determines the story that it tells. For instance, drawing a line at age 40 reveals only a minimal generation gap over time. The same trend is in evidence in the 18–24 versus 45–64 comparisons—but with a few exceptions. In six of the thirteen elections, including all from 1992–2000, the under/over 40 comparisons reveal younger voters to be more *Republican*.

However, these three instances do make intuitive sense when we consider theories of generational socialization. For example, in the 1960 election many of the voters in the 45–64 age group were young adults during the Great Depression, so we should expect them to be especially likely to vote Democratic. On the other hand, people aged 21–24 (18- to 20-year-olds were naturally excluded from the analysis before the passage of the Twenty-Sixth Amendment) were socialized into politics during the quiet 1950s Eisenhower era.

The result of their formative experiences logically could be lower rates of Democratic voting, especially when compared with their elders, who were socialized during the Great Depression and the presidency of Franklin D. Roosevelt.

What does this analysis ultimately tell us? Our results offer some support for the political significance of life cycle effects on voting behavior. That is, the youngest voters are the most liberal (as captured loosely by Democratic voting), but this effect appears to evaporate with age—and the increased income and homeownership that tend to accompany advancing age. At the same time, due to the variation across the years, it is impossible to conclude definitively that partisan attachments are completely stable over time. The electorate is alive both literally and figuratively. Voters respond to issues and significant events as they arise. That said, age groups do appear to have some set points—perhaps shaped by generational socialization experiences—that seem to vary only slightly in the short term.

It is an indisputable fact that the generation gap has narrowed over time. As we have noted, however, the size of this gap is partially a function of how we calculate it, as well as how we examine generations. Studying the effect of age on voting behavior by dividing the electorate into two groups yields simple, concrete conclusions, but may miss part of the *real story* of how age affects voting. Thus, we now turn to more nuanced examinations of intergenerational differences in voting behavior.

THE GENERATION GAP IN 2004

The generation gap did not grab headlines during the 2004 presidential campaign. In an election dominated by discussion of the war in Iraq and national security concerns, generational differences in political preference were not emphasized. However, while there was no talk of candidates vying over "canasta grandmas" to accompany the discussion of "NASCAR dads," "security moms," and "values voters," candidates did pay some attention to the age factor. Both campaigns expressed a desire to capture the "youth vote." Controversy arose when the powerful American Association of Retired Persons (AARP) endorsed Kerry in 2004 in large part due to the group's dissatisfaction with the Medicare reform bill George W. Bush signed the previous year.[19] The candidates also engaged in an ongoing war of words over age-relevant issues such as health care and prescription drugs.[20]

To what extent were there discernable electoral divisions along generational lines in 2004? Using the 2004 American National Election Study (ANES), Table 8.1 reports the size of the so-called "generation gap" in the presidential vote by comparing voters over the age of 40 to those under 40. This age gap is calculated in two ways: first, as the difference in the percentage of support for Kerry between those over and under 40, and second, as the difference in the net vote for George W. Bush between these same two categories.

TABLE 8.1   THE GENERATION GAP IN 2004 BY THE OVER 40/UNDER 40 SPLIT
(PERCENT VOTING FOR BUSH AND KERRY)

	18–40	41+	TOTAL	Under/Over
John Kerry	53.73	47.07	49.36	40 Gap by
George Bush	46.27	52.93	50.64	% for
				Kerry:
				6.7
Net for Bush	–7.46	+5.86	+1.28	Under/Over
% of voters	34.36	65.64	100.00	40 Gap by
				net for
				Bush:
				–1.6

Note: Votes for Ralph Nader and other minor-party candidates have been excluded from the analysis.
$\chi^2(1)=3.1227; p=0.077$.

Source: American National Election Study, 2004 (N=780).

Looking quickly at the vote totals reported in Table 8.1, we see that the 2004 ANES sample is close to the official national popular vote totals, where Bush won 50.73 percent of the vote to Kerry's 48.27 percent.[21] Turning to the over-40/under-40 division, the big story is how small the gap appears (regardless of how it is presented). Looking at the percentage of the vote for Kerry, the difference is modest; younger voters voted for the Senator at slightly higher rates than their elders. When we examine the generation gap using the difference in the net vote for Bush, it appears practically nonexistent (at just 1.6 percentage points), and at first glance appears to be incorrectly signed because the over 40/under 40 division actually favors Kerry.

Table 8.2 makes sense of this apparent discrepancy, reporting the percentage of the presidential vote for Bush and Kerry within four age groups: 18–24, 25–44, 45–64, and 65+. Table 8.2 also reports the net percentage of the

TABLE 8.2   THE GENERATION GAP IN THE 2004 PRESIDENTIAL VOTE BY AGE GROUP
(PERCENT VOTING FOR BUSH AND KERRY)

	18–24	25–44	45–64	65+	TOTAL
John Kerry	62.5	50.0	45.4	51.1	49.4
George Bush	37.5	50.0	54.6	48.9	50.6
Net for Bush	–25.0	0.0	+9.1	–2.2	+1.3
% of voters	8.2	33.3	40.6	17.8	100.0

Note: Votes for Ralph Nader and other minor-party candidates have been excluded from the analysis.
$\chi^2(3)=6.5906; p=0.086$.

Source: American National Election Study, 2004 (N=780).

vote for Bush within each age category as well as the percentage of the electorate comprised by each age group. Here we see that Kerry dominated the youth vote in 2004, besting Bush by 25 percentage points among those aged 18–24. However, Bush's victory can be explained by the fact that 18- to 24-year-olds constitute less than 10 percent of the electorate. By comparison, 25- to 44-year-olds comprise about one-third of the electorate; 45- to 64-year-olds (mostly Baby Boomers) account for fully 40 percent; individuals over 65 constitute roughly 18 percent. Although 25- to 44-year-olds split their votes between the two candidates roughly equally, Bush carried the largest age group—the 45- to 64-year-old vote—handily. Kerry clearly appealed to the oldest and youngest members of the electorate, but this appeal was not enough for him to win the election.

Was this large difference between the young and not so young unique to the 2004 election, or have similarly sized gaps been present over many elections? Recall that Figure 8.4 shows that the 2004 gap between the young and those in late middle age was rivaled in size only in 1972. Interestingly, 1972 was another wartime election as well as the first election in which 18- to 20-year-olds could vote. A sizable gap also existed in 2000 and in 1992, though neither of these was quite as large as the current one. We will investigate the reasons for this pattern in the next section.

How did the intergenerational vote breakdown for Kerry compare to the age gaps in previous elections? People aged 25–44 voted for Kerry at about the same rate as was the case in 2000, but this level of support was down seven points from the election and reelection of Clinton in 1992 and 1996 (see Figure 8.3). As noted above, Kerry really lost ground to Bush among members of the 45- to 64-year-old group: he received less than 45 percent of their votes, which was down nearly 10 percent from what Gore received from the same age group in 2000, and even lower than the support Clinton received in 1992 and 1996. Finally, while voters aged 65 and above voted for Kerry at about the same rate they did for Gore in 2000, Clinton enjoyed about five more percentage points of support in both of his elections. However, the 2004 Democratic voting rate among people aged 65 and above was *greater* than it was during the election and reelection of Reagan in 1980 and 1984. This is a logical finding since many people who were over 65 in the 1980s were socialized in the *pre-New Deal* period, which was an era of Republican strength in American politics.

EXPLAINING THE GENERATION GAP IN 2004

Thus far we have pointed out some generational differences in the 2004 vote, and we have placed these differences in the context of historical trends. But what broad forces explain these results? What drove Americans' vote choices in 2004, and did different sets of factors matter more for older versus younger voters?

Drawing on conventional political wisdom and life cycle theories, one way in which we might expect age differences to have mattered in 2004 is through the importance that different age groups place on specific issues based on self-interest. For example, older voters often pay more taxes than younger voters and are more concerned about Social Security and Medicare health care benefits.[22] We would therefore expect opinions on social welfare issues to be more important determinants of the vote for older voters than for younger voters.

Another possible explanation might be opinions about the war in Iraq and national security concerns, as these were the predominant issues of the campaign. We would expect that people who approved of Bush's handling of the war would be more likely to vote for him. Likewise, we would expect that people who felt that Bush had made the United States more secure would vote to retain him in office. If there are sizable differences in opinion on these issues across age groups, we might have discovered a viable explanation for the modest generation gap in 2004. Because older voters have lived through other times when the nation was at war, security concerns might be especially salient to them, which might predispose them to vote for Bush.

Figure 8.5 presents opinions on Bush's handling of the Iraq war by the four age groups. A quick glance reveals few sizable differences across generations. Although 18- to 24-year-olds were more likely than any other age group to disapprove of Bush's handling of the war in Iraq, this disapproval was

FIGURE 8.5   APPROVAL OF BUSH'S HANDLING OF THE WAR IN IRAQ BY AGE GROUP, 2004 (PERCENTS)

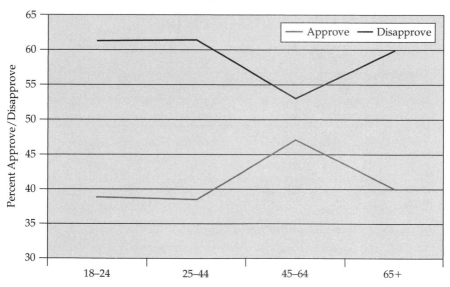

Source: American National Election Study, 2004.

nearly matched by that of 25- to 44-year-olds *and* that of people over 65 years of age. And while a higher percentage of 45- to 64-year-olds approved of Bush's handling of the war, a majority within this age group still disapproved.

What about opinions on Bush and national security? We find a strong relationship between Americans' views about national security and their opinions of Bush's handling of the war in Iraq, but the two questions do not overlap perfectly.[23] Thus, in Figure 8.6 we see that less than a quarter of all Americans felt that the United States was *less* secure under the Bush administration; this view is about the same across age groups. Although the youngest age group was most likely to say that Bush had made the United States *less* secure, this percentage was just barely higher than the percentage reported for 25- to 44-year-olds and only a few points higher than that reported for those over 45. However, the gap between the youngest voters and those aged 45–64 approached 15 percent, which is sizable. While young people may not necessarily think the United States has become less secure, fewer of them think it is *more* secure when compared to voters in their parents' age group (45–64). Overall, these quick examinations reveal few easily distinguishable generational patterns, which squares well with previous studies that find limited evidence supporting the assumption that young people are less likely to support military action than older people.[24] Our findings also suggest that the war in Iraq and national security issues should be thought to have had *period* effects in 2004; these two issues affected Americans across generations.

Finally, we consider the other major focus of the 2004 presidential campaign: "values." Some have argued that the values debate mattered a great

FIGURE 8.6   OPINIONS BY AGE ON WHETHER THE BUSH ADMINISTRATION HAS MADE THE U.S. MORE OR LESS SECURE

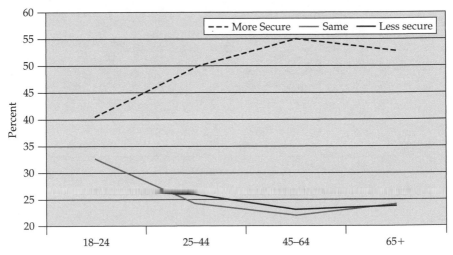

Source: American National Election Study, 2004.

deal on Election Day.[25] Others have focused on how the issue of same-sex marriage increased turnout in the 11 states with proposed marriage amendments on their ballots, influencing the ultimate electoral outcome.[26] Although both presidential candidates officially supported defining marriage as the union of one man and one woman, Bush went further than Kerry on this issue by supporting the creation of a federal constitutional amendment banning same-sex marriage. Thus, we might expect individuals who ardently favor same-sex marriage to have voted for the less conservative Kerry and those who vehemently oppose same-sex marriage to have voted for the more conservative Bush.

Were there sizable generational differences in opinion on same-sex marriage? Figure 8.7 presents approval of same-sex marriage by age group. Notice that while a majority of all Americans oppose same-sex marriage, a slight majority of the youngest age group approve of the idea. Rates of approval decline substantially as we move from the youngest Americans to the oldest. Clearly, there appear to be large generational distinctions on this issue, with the youngest (18–24) and second youngest (25–44) groups of voters approving of same-sex marriage at higher rates—voters who grew up in times in which homosexuality was more openly discussed, debated, and adopted into popular culture.[27]

We now turn to a more systematic test using a procedure (logistic regression) that allows us to gauge the effect of a variety of factors (simultaneously) on an individual's vote choice. We are especially interested to see if the factors that influenced younger voters (aged 18–40) were different than those that

FIGURE 8.7   APPROVAL OF SAME-SEX MARRIAGE BY AGE GROUP, 2004 (PERCENTS)

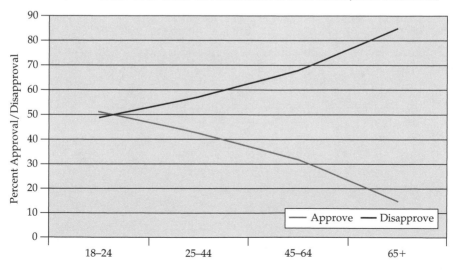

Source: American National Election Study, 2004.

affected older voters (aged 40 and above). Were individuals in different age groups motivated by different considerations when casting their votes? The results of our analysis are presented in Table 8.3; additional details on the variables can be found in the Appendix to this chapter.

For 18- to 40-year-olds, the only issues that exerted a significant effect on vote choice were (1) their opinion about Bush's job of handling the war in Iraq and (2) their views on whether Bush had improved national security. Not surprisingly, increased support for the Bush administration on both of these fronts made one more likely to vote for Bush. And as we would expect, high income and Republican Party identification also made individual voters more likely

TABLE 8.3   PREDICTING THE VOTE IN 2004 FOR VOTERS UNDER 40 VERSUS VOTERS OVER 40

	18–40 YEAR-OLDS		**41+** YEAR-OLDS		SIGNIFICANTLY
ISSUES	B	S.E.	B	S.E.	DIFFERENT?
Social welfare	−0.82	0.71	1.38***	0.39	+
War/national security	−3.33***	1.04	−2.32***	0.45	
National economy	−0.56	0.62	0.03	0.38	
Same-sex marriage	0.36	1.12	1.03†	0.69	
Personal finances	−0.22	0.65	−0.13	0.35	
Abortion	−0.79	0.65	−0.17	0.38	
CONTROLS					
Partisanship	2.38***	0.80	1.46***	0.40	
Ideology	0.76	0.80	−0.08	0.53	
Political interest	−0.45	0.48	0.23	0.37	
Non-White	−4.52**	1.74	−1.8**	0.78	†
Female	1.47	1.14	0.05	0.61	
Education	−0.36	0.71	0.71*	0.40	
Income	1.54**	0.64	−0.23	0.41	+
Constant	0.97	1.2	−0.52	0.62	
N	170		294		
−2 log likelihood	−18.8		−43.58		
LR χ^2	197.91***		316.93***		
Pseudo-R^2	0.84		0.78		

Source: American National Election Study, 2004 all coefficients standardized. † $p<0.10$ (one-tailed test); † $p<0.05$ (two-tailed test); *$p<0.10$; **$p<0.05$; ***$p<0.01$ (two-tailed test); 1=Bush; 0=Kerry.

to vote for Bush. The only other factor that affected younger voters' choice between Bush and Kerry was race: not surprisingly, non-Whites were significantly less likely to vote for Bush.

For voters over 40, several factors worked in the same way as they did for younger voters. Stronger Republicans again were more likely to vote for Bush, as were Whites. While income level did not exert a significant effect on the vote choice of older individuals, opinions on the war in Iraq and national security were important considerations and worked in the same way as they did for younger voters. There is also tentative evidence that opposition to same-sex marriage was an important consideration for people over 40 who voted for Bush. Moreover, support for social welfare (desiring more government services, national health insurance, and government guarantees of available jobs) was an important criterion for people over 40 who voted for Kerry, and was nearly as strong a consideration for members of this age group as their views on the war. This finding may be indicative of a new life cycle effect, as well-paying industrial jobs have deserted large portions of the United States, leaving many middle-aged people feeling less secure about their financial future than in years past.

Taking a long view, we see one more life cycle effect at work. Younger voters are just entering the political system, largely without a history of concerns and expectations about government. Older voters, on the other hand, are more likely to have a wider array of concerns as their lives unfold (especially after they finish formal schooling) through their professions, neighborhoods, and personal life circumstances (especially health and wealth). Our results show older voters employing a broader set of considerations than younger voters. Perhaps we can conclude that younger voters might be more likely to respond when one issue dominates a campaign, while older voters might be less likely to make their voting choice in response to a singular concern.

To better illustrate the substance of these findings, Figure 8.8 presents the probability that a "typical" White, pro-choice voter would cast a vote for Bush in 2004. The probabilities are calculated from a logistic regression analysis similar to the one described above, and show what happens when we hold all personal and opinion characteristics constant (see the bottom of Figure 8.8 for a complete description of the "baseline" voter profile), but vary age for Republicans, Independents, and Democrats. A value above 0.5 means that an individual is more likely to vote for Bush, and a value under 0.5 means that an individual is more likely to vote for Kerry.

A quick first glance at Figure 8.8 reminds us that the 2004 election was a close contest fought largely along party lines. It also reinforces the story that we have been telling thus far, namely, that the generation gap was relatively small in 2004, and that few of the factors that truly structured the electorate's vote differed along generational lines. Figure 8.8 clearly shows that regardless of age, Republicans were more likely to vote for Bush and Democrats more likely to vote for Kerry (holding other factors at set values).[28] This should come as no surprise, but let us consider Independents, who hover around the 0.4 mark, which

FIGURE 8.8   PROBABILITY OF VOTING FOR BUSH IN 2004, VARYING AGE

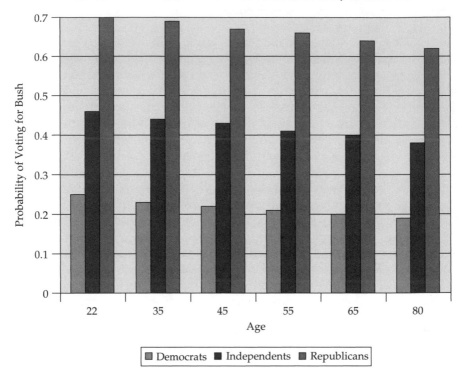

Source: American National Election Study, 2004.

means that their vote overall was close to a 50–50 toss-up. Across all age groups, Independents leaned slightly toward Kerry (their probability was just below 0.5), and this trend is more discernable as the voter profile gets older.

Figure 8.9 zeroes in on these critical swing voters, looking at the probability of a "typical" Independent casting a vote for Bush while varying age and opinions on social welfare,[29] the only factor besides income for which we discovered a significant age-related difference. This figure shows that most of the differences in the probability of voting for Bush are due to voters' views on social welfare—and *not* their age. To illustrate: the young (25-year-olds), the middle aged (50-year-olds), and the elderly (75-year-olds) are *all* more likely to vote for Kerry if they hold more liberal opinions on social welfare; likewise, all three age groups are more likely to vote for Bush if they are conservative on social welfare. For the most part, the same pattern holds for people with moderate views on social welfare, although we do observe a bit more age-based variation among moderates. Younger Independents holding moderate opinions on social welfare creep up toward the "toss-up" mark of 0.5, while older, moderate Independents become more likely to vote for Kerry.

FIGURE 8.9 PROBABILITY OF VOTING FOR BUSH IN 2004, POLITICAL INDEPENDENTS

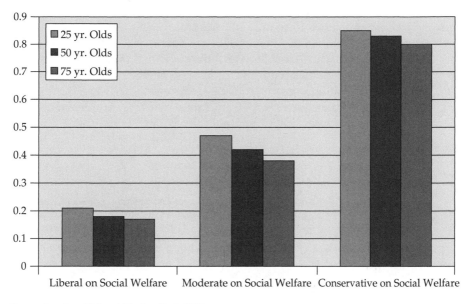

Source: American National Election Study, 2004.

CONCLUSION

The generation gap was modest at best in 2004, but this fact is not surprising in light of the fact that the presidential election took place during wartime. The war in Iraq and national security took center stage during the campaign, and our results demonstrate that views on these two issues were the most important considerations (aside from race) for the typical American voter. In fact, for both older and younger voters, opinion on these issues had a larger effect on vote choice than did partisanship, and as we demonstrated, there were few clearly discernable generational patterns in opinion on these issues. The lesson here is that period effects can be particularly potent, especially during wartime. This is a lesson that clearly was not lost on the Bush-Cheney reelection campaign in 2004.

Nevertheless, some age-related differences did surface in our analysis of this election. For one, income mattered a great deal in the voting decisions of younger voters, with the wealthier more likely to vote for Bush. Partisanship was also a strong predictor of the vote for the electorate as a whole, working in the same way for both old and young voters. As we discussed earlier (and presented in Figure 8.1), a good deal of research has indicated that partisan attitudes are acquired through the process of political socialization and solidified over the life course. We feel confident in concluding that generational effects were most evident in 2004 through partisan differences.

Finally, another expected intergenerational difference concerned views on social welfare. Opinions about the extent to which the government should provide public assistance to maintain a minimum standard of living had a significant effect on the voting choices of older Americans, even after accounting for their views on the war in Iraq and the perennial pull of partisanship. Younger voters, on the other hand, were far less concerned about social welfare issues. Given that the American electorate is aging, we can expect social welfare issues to become even more important in electoral politics, with candidates vying for the votes of the graying Baby Boom Generation.

NOTES

[1]Robert D. Putnam, "Tuning In, Tuning Out: The Strange Disappearance of Social Capital in America," in *Controversies in Voting Behavior*, 4th ed., eds. Richard G. Niemi and Herbert Weisberg (Washington, DC: CQ Press, 2001).

[2]For more on differences in turnout rates between younger and older voters, see Martin P. Wattenberg, *Where Have All the Voters Gone?* (Cambridge, MA: Harvard University Press, 2002); Martin P. Wattenberg, *Is Voting for Young People?* (New York: Pearson Longman, 2007).

[3]Stanley W. Moore, James Lare, and Kenneth A. Wagner, *The Child's Political World* (New York: Praeger, 1985).

[4]Richard M. Merelman, *Political Socialization and Educational Climates* (New York: Holt, 1971).

[5]M. Kent Jennings and Gregory B. Markus, "Partisan Orientations over the Long Haul: Results from the Three-Wave Political Socialization Panel Study," *American Political Science Review* 78 (1984): 1000–1018; M. Kent Jennings and Richard G. Niemi, *The Political Character of Adolescence* (Princeton, NJ: Princeton University Press, 1974).

[6]Paul A. Beck, "The Role of Agents in Political Socialization," in *Handbook of Political Socialization*, ed. Stanley A. Renshon (New York: Free Press, 1977).

[7]Robert S. Erikson and Kent Tedin, *American Public Opinion*, 7th ed. (New York: Pearson Longman, 2005).

[8]Philip E. Converse, *The Dynamics of Party Support: Cohort-Analyzing Party Identification* (Beverly Hills, CA: Sage, 1976).

[9]Theodore Rosenof, *Realignment: The Theory that Changed the Way We Think about American Politics* (New York: Rowman and Littlefield, 2003).

[10]V. O. Key, "A Theory of Critical Elections," *Journal of Politics* 17 (1955): 3–18. However, Key backed away from this view just four years after the publication of this study, allowing an element of gradual change to compliment or replace critical shifts: see V. O. Key, "Secular Realignment and the Party System," *Journal of Politics* 21 (1959): 198–210.

[11]See John H. Aldrich and Richard G. Niemi, "The Sixth American Party System: Electoral Change, 1952–1992," in *Controversies in Voting Behavior*, 4th ed., eds. Richard G. Niemi and Herbert Weisberg (Washington, DC: CQ Press, 2001); Walter Dean Burnham, *Critical Elections and the Mainspring of American Politics* (New York: Norton, 1970); James L. Sundquist, *Dynamics of the Party System: Alignment and Realignment of the Political Parties in the United States* (Washington, DC: Brookings Institution, 1983).

[12]William H. Flanigan and Nancy H. Zingale, *Political Behavior of the American Electorate*, 11th ed. (Washington, DC: CQ Press, 2006): 94.

[13]See Erikson and Tedin (2005).

[14]See Jennings and Markus (1984).

[15]M. Kent Jennings, "Residuals of a Movement: The Aging American Protest Generation," *American Political Science Review* 81 (1987): 365–381.

[16]Robert S. Erikson, Michael B. MacKuen, and James A. Stimson, *The Macro Polity* (New York: Cambridge University Press, 2002).

[17]This term was coined by Tom Brokaw, *The Greatest Generation* (New York: Random House, 1998).

[18]Our analysis includes the vote percentage for the Democratic and Republican parties only (i.e., third parties are excluded from the analysis).

[19]Jonathan Finer, "Kerry Courts Seniors in Nevada," *Washington Post* (August 11, 2004): A6.

[20]Elisabeth Bumiller and David Halbfinger, "Bush and Kerry, Feeling Like Winners, Go to Las Vegas," *New York Times* (October 15, 2004): A21; Robert Pear and Carl Hulse, "Medicare Costs Are New Focus for Candidates," *New York Times* (September 12, 2004): A1.

[21]Ralph Nader won 0.38 percent of the popular vote in 2004. The official report of the Federal Election Commission, including vote totals for House and Senate races, is available online at http://www.fec.gov/pubrec/fe2004/federalelections2004.pdf.

[22]Andrea Louise Campbell, *How Policies Make Citizens: Senior Political Activism and the American Welfare State* (Princeton, NJ: Princeton University Press, 2003).

[23]The correlation between opinion on Bush's handling of the war in Iraq and whether Bush has made the United States more secure is 0.63 ($p<0.001$).

[24]Erikson and Tedin (2005): 194.

[25]Alan Abramowitz, "Terrorism, Gay Marriage and Incumbency: Explaining the Republican Victory in the 2004 Election," *The Forum* 2 (2004): Article 3.

[26]Gregory B. Lewis, "Same-Sex Marriage and the 2004 Presidential Election," *PS: Political Science and Politics* 38 (2005): 195–199.

[27]These findings are consistent with previous research on public opinion about homosexuality in general. See Jeni Loftus, "America's Liberalization in Attitudes toward Homosexuality, 1973 to 1998," *American Sociological Review* 66 (2001): 762–782.

[28]In Figure 8.8, we hold demographic characteristics and opinions on a host of other factors constant. The predicted probabilities were created with CLARIFY. The baseline is a white, ideologically moderate, somewhat politically interested, pro-gay marriage, pro-choice individual with a moderate (10) opinion on the "social welfare" item, mean opinion on "war/national security,"mean levels of education and income, and who reported that both the national economy and their personal economic situations have not changed. Democrats are strong and weak Democrats; Republicans are strong and weak Republicans; Independents are "pure" independents and "leaners." (Please see the appendix for full variable coding.)

[29]In Figure 8.9, we hold demographic characteristics and opinions on a host of other factors constant. Predicted probabilities were created with CLARIFY. Political Independents include leaning Republicans and Democrats. The baseline is a white, ideologically moderate, somewhat politically interested, pro-gay marriage, pro-choice individual with mean levels of education and income, mean opinion on the "war/national security" item, and who reported that both the national economy and their personal economic situations have not changed. Liberal on social welfare = 3 on the additive index; moderate on social welfare = 10; conservative on social welfare = 21. (Please see the appendix for full variable coding.)

APPENDIX

VARIABLE CODING

Abortion: Respondent's opinion on abortion: 1=by law, abortion should never be permitted; 2=the law should permit abortion only in the case of rape, incest, or when the woman's life is in danger; 3=the law should permit abortion for reasons other than rape, incest, or danger to the woman's life, but only after the need for the abortion has been clearly established; 4=by law, a woman should always be able to obtain an abortion as a matter of personal choice.

Age: years, 18–90. The continuous measure of age was used to divide the sample into those 18–40/41+, and into various age groups.

Education: Number of years of school completed, from 1–17 or more.

Same-Sex Marriage: Respondent's position on same-sex marriage. 1=not allowed; 0=allowed.

Gender: 1=female; 0=male.

Ideology: 1=extremely liberal; 2=liberal; 3=slightly liberal; 4=moderate; 5=slightly conservative; 6=conservative; 7=extremely conservative.

Income: Yearly household income in 23 categories, from less than $2,999 to over $120,000.

National Economy: Respondent's assessment of the national economy over the past four years. 1=much better; 2=somewhat better; 3=same; 4=somewhat worse; 5=much worse.

Party Identification: 0=strong Democrat; 1=weak Democrat; 2=independent leaning Democrat; 3=independent; 4=independent leaning Republican; 5=weak Republican; 6=strong Republican.

Personal Finances: How much better/worse is the respondent and his/her family compared to a year ago? 1=much better; 2=somewhat better; 3=same; 4=somewhat worse; 5=much worse.

Political Interest: How interested is the respondent in political campaigns? 1=very much interested; 3=somewhat interested; 5=not much interested.

Presidential Vote in 2004: 1=voted for Bush; 0=voted for Kerry.

Race: 0=White; 1=non-White.

Religious attendance: How often the respondent attends religious services: 1=never; 2=a few times a year; 3=once or twice a month; 4=almost every week; 5=every week.

Social Welfare: An additive measure running from 3–21 combining opinions on items asking about the government's role in providing jobs and a standard of living, the government's role in providing insurance, and whether the government should provide more or fewer services: 3=most liberal on social welfare issues; 21=most conservative on social welfare issues ($\alpha = 0.71$).

War/National Security: An additive measure running from 2–9 combining items on approval of Bush's handling of the war in Iraq and whether the Bush administration has made the United States more or less secure: 2=most support for Bush administration; 9=least support for the Bush administration ($\alpha = 0.78$).

9

TARGETING AND ELECTORAL GAPS

❧

ANNA GREENBERG

People who run political campaigns spend a great deal of time thinking about how to reach voters and what to say to them. This process is called "targeting." Campaigns engage in targeting largely to increase the efficiency of their communication with voters. Rarely can a campaign simply afford to "talk to everyone," so the campaign has to determine which voters should be given priority. Strategic targeting helps campaigns categorize voters for the purposes of getting core supporters to the polls or persuading key voter groups to vote in a particular way. Every campaign, large and small, relies on targeting to determine who should receive paid communications (through television advertising, direct mail, and e-mail) and who should be contacted in person (through phone calls, canvasses, and house parties).

Campaigns use a variety of criteria and technology for determining the voter groups they will target. Such criteria include geography, demographic and social characteristics, and political history. For instance, campaigns might target voters in suburban areas, older women, or partisans with a history of voting in congressional elections. Campaigns employ a wide range of technologies to determine the specific groups of citizens they ought to target, including voter identification programs, survey research, and data mining and micro-targeting.

Targeting voters in campaigns is not a new development; just think back to the machine politics of the Nineteenth Century when party bosses brought their supporters to the polls with a variety of unsavory means. The rise of mass media in politics—and particularly the dawn of television advertising—removed campaigns' focus on direct contact with voters to some degree. In recent years, however, we have seen a lively and invigorated discussion of voter targeting, in part because of advances in data collection, software development, and computer processing. Moreover, the growing fragmentation of media and resulting difficulty of reaching voters with traditional television advertising increasingly require campaigns to place an even greater emphasis on direct voter contact, and consequently, a greater investment in field activities.

Both Republicans and Democrats are working hard to refine their targeting methodologies, leading to greater investment in list development and modeling, or what some call "micro-targeting." The idea of micro-targeting is to create personalized and customized voter contact strategies for individual campaigns. The goal is to develop a strategy by which the campaign may speak directly to the concerns of very narrowly defined groups of voters. This narrowcast targeting allows campaigns to cobble together a coalition of disparate voter groups to get the votes of "50 percent plus 1," resulting in a win, on Election Day.

TARGETING BASE SUPPORTERS AND PERSUADABLE VOTERS

Campaigns have two tasks: getting their supporters out to vote and persuading voters to vote for their candidate. Some analysts argue that a campaigns' primary need is to get their base supporters to the polls, a theory espoused most prominently by George W. Bush's political advisor, Karl Rove, after the 2000 presidential election. Indeed, the Republican Party spent much of its time between the 2000 and 2004 presidential elections consolidating its base of most reliable supporters, primarily through the work of volunteers in local communities (most notably in conservative churches).[1] In both 2002 and 2004, Republicans were able to increase turnout significantly among key groups of their supporters, such as White evangelical Protestants.[2]

Ultimately, however, the idea that campaigns choose between activating base and persuadable voters represents a false choice. It is extremely difficult to win elections without receiving solid support from base supporters *and* competing for—and winning—the votes of at least some persuadable voters. Of course, in states or districts that are skewed toward a particular political party, it is more important to ensure that one's own partisans vote. On the other hand, in states or districts where voters are divided more equally between the two parties, targeting efforts need to concentrate equally on persuadable voters.[3] Campaigns must make sure they find the right mathematical combination of base voters and persuadable voters *and* customize their targeting plans to respond to the dynamics of their district or state.

BASE VOTERS

"Base voters" form the core of a candidate's support. Most campaigns begin by determining the scope of their base support. In the early stages of a campaign, these voters also may be recruited as volunteers or provide campaign contributions. Ultimately, however, making sure these core supporters turn out to vote is the campaign's most important task. Mobilizing voters requires specialized kinds of communication, focused not so much on persuading people to vote for a particular candidate, but the importance of voting itself.[4]

It is a well-established fact that partisanship is the most important determinant of support for any candidate. Despite the general decline in party identification and the corresponding rise in political independence, partisanship remains the most important predictor of the vote in any election.[5] Moreover, while the number of self-identified Independents has grown, so has the number of strong partisans. Crossover voting (ticket-splitting) is now relatively rare. Most campaigns know that they need to win the vast majority of their partisans if they want to achieve victory. Generally, if more than 15–20 percent of partisans are not supporting candidates of their party, the campaign has a real "base" problem.

Determining the scope of partisan support can be relatively straightforward; many states record "party registration" as part of their voter registration process. List vendors and state party organizations maintain up-to-date lists of voters' party registration and voting history (including participation in primary elections, which can be essential to finding intense partisans). Armed with this information, campaigns can contact voters who identify with their party—particularly those who have a strong history of voting in elections. They also can locate their partisan support geographically by examining precinct-level data and identifying the precincts in which their party's candidates tend to do the best.

Targeting supporters based on partisanship alone also has limitations. First, many states neither require nor offer party registration as part of their registration process. State party organizations and campaigns can augment voter lists in these states in an effort to capture partisanship with information such as participation in party primaries or voter identification ("IDs") information collected by telephone or via door-to-door canvass. However, these methods are imperfect, and generally miss large groups of partisans. Second, some states have large numbers of Independents or people who do not register with any party. Given that in the United States people cast their vote with a secret ballot, it is very difficult to determine if such voters have a particular partisan bent.

Campaigns generally layer additional information over partisanship to help overcome these gaps and the lack of precision that comes from targeting by party alone. Certain demographic groups have a history of voting for candidates from particular parties (see Table 9.1).[6] For example, African Americans and Jewish Americans are considered reliable Democratic voters,[7] while White evangelical Protestants regularly cast their vote for Republicans. Other groups are considered close to being base supporters, even if they give candidates slightly narrower margins of victory. Close to two-thirds of unmarried women cast their lot with Democrats for at least three election cycles, while White, blue-collar men are reliably Republican—unless they are union members.[8]

TABLE 9.1   CONGRESSIONAL VOTES OF BASE GROUPS

	2002	2004	2006
African Americans	90–9	89–10	89–10
Jewish Americans	62–35	76–22	87–12
White evangelical Protestants	21–77	25–74	29–70
Unmarried women	60–39*	60–34	66–32
White blue-collar married men**	28–69	36–53	31–68

*Democracy Corps/Campaign for America's Future national post-election survey conducted in 2002. The survey, which was conducted from November 5–6, reached 1,992 registered voters.

**Democracy Corps/Campaign for America's Future national post-election surveys conducted in 2002, 2004, and 2006. The 2004 survey, which was conducted from November 2–3, reached 2,000 registered voters. The 2006 survey was conducted from November 7–8 and reached 1,011 registered voters. "White blue-collar married men" are white married men under 50 years of age who do not have a four-year college degree.

Source: National Election Polls 2002, 2004, 2006. Figures shown are vote splits between Democrats and Republicans (D–R).

Obviously, there is overlap between a candidate's partisans and these demographic groups. Both African Americans and Jewish Americans tend to identify as Democrats, while White evangelical Protestants tend to identify with the Republican Party. These patterns of base support, whether based on partisanship or demographics, tend to be relatively stable over time. We know that partisanship changes slowly and occurs largely through generational replacement.[9]

Campaigns armed with a good understanding of history can make safe assumptions about the makeup of their core support. At the same time, patterns can change in response to political events and campaign strategies, even if partisanship remains relatively stable (see Table 9.2). White married women (the so-called "security moms") reliably cast their lot with the Republicans in 2002 and 2004, but Democrats picked up some of their support in 2006, largely as a response to the war in Iraq. While White evangelical Protestants voted reliably for Republican candidates in the 1980s and 1990s, Karl Rove worked successfully to further increase Republican margins among this group of base voters through a focus on socio-moral issues such as same-sex marriage and stem cell research.

TABLE 9.2   CONGRESSIONAL VOTE: CORE REPUBLICAN SUPPORT

	2002	2004	2006
White married women	41–56	39–54	44–55
White evangelical Protestants	21–77	25–74	29–70

Source: National Election Polls 2002, 2004, 2006; and Democracy Corps/Campaign for America's Future post-election surveys. Figures shown are vote splits between Democrats and Republicans (D–R).

Given that there is always some variability in base support, campaigns cannot rely solely on historical patterns and trends to make targeting decisions. To the extent that they can afford to pay for it, campaigns map their core support using survey research and other voter identification methods. Using surveys, campaigns identify base voters by asking a variety of questions:

1. *Strong supporters:* Campaign surveys often ask respondents about the strength of their support for both their own candidate and their opponent. A candidate's strong supporters comprise one pillar of the campaign's base vote.
2. *"Know them and like them":* Campaign surveys always ask respondents if they have heard of the candidates and if they like them. Identifying voters who know and like a candidate helps the campaign identify base support.
3. *"Dislike opponent":* Some candidates engender hostile responses from voters. Identifying the groups that dislike the opposing candidate but do not yet support the campaign's own candidate helps to identify potential base support.

Persuadable Voters

In seriously contested elections, candidates not only need to make sure their own "base" supporters make it to the polls on Election Day, but also need to persuade "swing" voters to support them. Only in the most conservative and liberal states and districts may candidates rely solely on getting their base supporters to the polls. Persuadable voters are more difficult to identify than base supporters because by definition they are not well defined ideologically. Persuadable voters are also often hard to cast in demographic terms, and often they are not concentrated in any one geographical area.

Voter lists can be useful in identifying persuadable or "swing" voters. Certainly, if a state voter file includes party registration, anyone who lacks a party preference or has registered as an Independent is a potential persuadable voter. On the other hand, Independents are not necessarily nonideological. As the authors of *The Myth of the Independent Voter* argue, self-identified Independents who say they lean toward a political party are often surprisingly loyal party voters.[10] Moreover, Independent voters sometimes break heavily for one party, as was the case in the 2006 congressional elections. Ultimately, campaigns need more information about these voters if they are going to customize their communications with them with any precision or efficiency.

Political geography represents one route to customizing communication with persuadable voters. Some campaigns examine partisan performance in specific geographic areas, usually at the precinct level, to determine if they can find untapped potential support. For example, the National Committee for an Effective Congress (NCEC), an organization allied with the Democratic

Party, gathers extensive political information at the county and precinct levels across the country. Using NCEC targeting information, campaigns are able to target infrequent voters who live in Democratic-leaning areas on the assumption that such voters will be open to Democratic campaign appeals.[11]

Looking beyond partisanship and geography, campaigns often examine historical voting patterns. There are groups of voters who tend either to divide evenly between the two parties in election after election or tend to be more variable in their voter preferences (see Table 9.3). Catholics, suburban voters, and seniors have been three of the most important "swing" groups in early twenty-first-century elections. These three groups are often "cross-pressured," meaning that they hold both liberal and conservative positions on a range of issues and therefore do not fall neatly into either partisan camp. Seniors, for example, are often socially conservative (for example, a majority oppose same-sex marriage), but are also deeply concerned about their economic security (and therefore support Social Security and Medicare). Suburban voters often are socially liberal (they are largely pro-choice and in favor of gun control) but also tax-sensitive.

Because they are not anchored by ideology and partisanship, persuadable voters tend to move more in response to current events. It is essential for any campaign to understand the context of its *current* political contest—and to avoid focusing solely on partisanship, geography, and history—to identify persuadable voters. The war in Iraq, for example, moved Independents heavily into the Democratic camp in 2006 after dividing them evenly between the two major parties in 2002 and 2004. In 2006 we also saw a number of Republican-leaning voters, particularly married women, shift their support to Democratic candidates, suggesting that they might be persuadable for both sides in the 2008 presidential election.

Survey research is a key tool for identifying persuadable voters. Campaigns use survey research to help identify persuadable voters and to understand how the dynamics of any individual race might influence persuadable voters. These surveys contain multiple indicators that help campaigns determine which voters are open to hearing more about a candidate or voting for

TABLE 9.3   CONGRESSIONAL VOTES OF PERSUADABLE GROUPS

	2002	2004	2006
Catholics	53–45	49–50	55–44
Suburban	40–57	48–51	51–48
Seniors	49–50	46–52	49–49
Independents	45–48	49–46	57–39
Married women	42–54	43–52	49–50

Source: National Election Polls 2002, 2004, 2006; and Democracy Corps/Campaign for America's Future 2002 post-election survey. Figures shown are vote splits between Democrats and Republicans (D–R).

that candidate. Campaigns often target four specific groups of persuadable voters. First, campaign surveys ask respondents for whom they intend to vote. *Undecided voters* constitute a clearly persuadable target group, although they are often a very small proportion of the people responding to a survey. Second, campaign surveys often ask respondents about the strength of their support for both their own candidate and the opponent. *Weak supporters* of a candidate or his or her opponent are potentially persuadable targets, as they tend to be less partisan and less informed. Third, *ticket splitters*—citizens who vote for candidates from both parties on the same ballot—clearly are persuadable targets, although some split-ticket voters may have a strong personal preference for voting for candidates of different parties. Finally, surveys often are designed to introduce information about candidates to voters with the goal of determining which voters move or change their preference. If large groups move or shift their expressed preferences over the course of a survey, the campaign will consider these *moveable voters* potential persuasion targets.

DEFINING VOTERS

Targeting base and persuadable voters requires campaigns to find ways of defining specific groups of voters, often quite narrowly. There are standard geographic and demographic indicators that pollsters and campaigns employ to segment the electorate. Some of these measures come from the voter lists maintained by list vendors and state party organizations, while others come from the survey research that is a standard component of most campaigns.

As mentioned above, campaigns categorize voters geographically. They employ geographic information to determine where to direct their communications and outreach within a given state or district. As a general rule, urban areas tend to lean Democratic while rural areas tend to lean Republican, with suburban areas often representing the battleground. Both parties work to increase turnout in urban and rural areas while fighting over the persuadable voters in the suburbs.

At the same time, each state and district has its own distinctive character, so a solid understanding of the political history of each particular place where the campaign wishes to garner support is essential. For example, the rural northern part of Minnesota actually represents a Democratic base, as this area has a long history of union activity associated with the mining industry. In Virginia, suburbs of Washington, DC, are heavily Democratic, reflecting the large concentration of federal employees who commute to work in the nation's capital. States such as South Dakota are almost entirely rural, so both parties have to target within a relatively homogenous electorate.

Measuring residence is fairly straightforward, as voter lists include geographic indicators down to the precinct level. When pollsters use voter lists, information on place of residence automatically becomes part of the survey

data. If pollsters use random-digit dialing (which is done when state voter
lists are not of a high enough quality to produce the representative random
sample required for a reliable survey), the resulting data will include geographic indicators such as county codes. These objective geographic measures also may be used with more subjective measures of the impact of
geography. For instance, understanding geographic mobility sometimes offers
clues to the changing political character of states or districts. Surveys can ask
respondents how long they have lived in their place of residence. Sometimes
newer residents exhibit distinct political behaviors compared with long-term
residents of the same locality.

Voter lists contain very limited demographic information, so targeting
with demographic variables nearly always requires survey research. Surveys
contain a standard set of demographic variables that analysts believe are associated with political outcomes, though the actual question wording often
varies from pollster to pollster (Figure 9.1 is an example of such demographic
questions). Nearly every survey conducted for a campaign will ask respondents about their gender, age, educational attainment, marital status, race,
and union membership. In some cases, pollsters further disaggregate these
demographic measures. For example, when pollsters ask a respondent's race,
many Hispanic voters identify as White or African American, so pollsters
often follow up with a question specifically designed to determine whether a
respondent is Hispanic. Surveys usually (but not always) include questions
about income level. Income is actually a less powerful predictor of political
behavior than educational attainment, however, which is fortunate for campaigns because many respondents refuse to answer survey questions about
their income.

FIGURE 9.1   SURVEY QUESTIONS: STANDARD DEMOGRAPHY QUESTIONS

Record respondent's gender (INTERVIEWER CODE—DO NOT ASK)
❑ 1 Male
❑ 2 Female

In what year were you born? (0000 = DON'T KNOW/REFUSED)

_____ 6 Enter Year

What is the last year of schooling that you have completed? (DO NOT READ LIST)

❑ 1 1–11th grade   ❑ 5 College graduate
❑ 2 High school graduate   ❑ 6 Post–graduate school
❑ 3 Noncollege post–H.S.   ❑ 7 (Don't know/Refused)
❑ 4 Some college

Are you married, single, separated, divorced, or widowed? (READ LIST)

❑ 1 Married
❑ 2 Single
❑ 3 Separated/divorced

❑ 4 Widowed
❑ 5 (Don't know/refused)

What racial or ethnic group best describes you? (READ LIST)

❑ 1 White
❑ 2 African-American or Black
❑ 3 Hispanic or Latino
❑ 4 Native American

❑ 5 Asian
❑ 6 (Other)
❑ 7 (Don't know/refused)

(SKIP IF HISPANIC OR LATINO IN ABOVE) Are you of Spanish or Hispanic origin or descent?

❑ 1 Yes
❑ 2 No
❑ 3 (Don't know/Refused)

Would you describe your Hispanic origin as Mexican, Puerto Rican, Cuban, Latin American, Central American, or Spanish?

❑ 1 Mexican
❑ 2 Puerto Rican
❑ 3 Cuban
❑ 4 Latin American

❑ 5 Central American
❑ 6 Spanish
❑ 7 (Other) (RECORD RESPONSE)
❑ 8 (Don't know/refused)

Are you a member of a labor union?

(IF NO) Is any member of your household a union member?

❑ 1 Yes: Respondent belongs
❑ 2 Household member

❑ 3 No member belongs
❑ 4 (Don't know/refused)

Last year, that is, in 2006, what was your total family income from all sources, before taxes? Just stop me when I get to the right category.

(READ LIST)

❑ 1 Less than $10,000
❑ 2 $10,000 to under $20,000
❑ 3 $20,000 to under $30,000
❑ 4 $30,000 to under $50,000
❑ 5 $50,000 to under $75,000

❑ 6 $75,000 to under $100,000
❑ 7 $100,000 or more
❑ 8 (Refused)
❑ 9 (Don't know)

Do you have any children 18 years of age or younger living at home?

❑ 1 Yes
❑ 2 No
❑ 3 (Don't know/refused)

Source: Greenberg, Quinlan Rosner Research.

There are other measures that relate more to behavior than ascribed characteristics such as gender and race that are of deep political import (see Figure 9.2). For example, in the West, it would be impossible to understand political dynamics without asking respondents about gun ownership. Another example surrounds religiosity, which constitutes one of the strongest dividing lines in American politics. Pollsters have a number of options available if they would like to learn about respondents' religiosity, as both worship attendance levels and religious affiliation are strong predictors of voting behavior.

FIGURE 9.2   SURVEY QUESTIONS: STANDARD SOCIAL CHARACTERISTICS

How many guns or rifles do you own? (DO NOT READ LIST)

❏ 1 None   ❏ 4 10 or more
❏ 2 1–2   ❏ 5 (Don't know/Refused)
❏ 3 3–9

What is your religion? (DO NOT READ LIST)

❏ 1 Protestant (INTERVIEWER—ACCEPT BAPTIST, LUTHERAN, METHODIST,
        EPISCOPAL, PRESBYTERIAN, CHRISTIAN, NONDENOMINATIONAL)
❏ 2 Catholic
❏ 3 Jewish
❏ 4 Muslim
❏ 5 (Other/none/refused)

(ASK IF PROTESTANT IN ABOVE) Which one of these words best describes your kind of Christianity—fundamentalist, evangelical, charismatic, Pentecostal, or moderate to liberal?

❏ 1 Fundamentalist   ❏ 4 Moderate to liberal
❏ 2 Evangelical   ❏ 5 (Something else)
❏ 3 Charismatic/Pentecostal   ❏ 6 (Don't know/refused)

How often do you attend religious services—every week, once or twice a month, several times a year, or hardly ever?

❏ 1 Every week   ❏ 4 Hardly ever
❏ 2 Once or twice a month   ❏ 5 (Never)
❏ 3 Several times a year   ❏ 6 (Don't know/Refused)

Source: Greenberg, Quinlan, Rosner Research.

Finally, every campaign survey must ask a standard set of political questions (see Figure 9.3), especially to assess respondents' partisanship and ideology. There are other, more nuanced measures, such as the respondent's partisan voting history, which help campaigns locate persuadable voters who have a history of voting for candidates of different parties. Understanding the respondents' general political bent helps campaigns understand in greater detail which groups of voters they ought to target.

FIGURE 9.3 SURVEY QUESTIONS: STANDARD POLITICAL MEASURES

Generally speaking, do you think of yourself as (ROTATE DEMOCRAT/REPUBLICAN) a Democrat, a Republican or what?

❏ 1 Democrat ❏ 4 (Other)
❏ 2 (Independent) ❏ 5 (Don't know/Refused)
❏ 3 Republican

(ASK IF DEMOCRAT/REPUBLICAN ABOVE) Would you call yourself a strong partisanship or a not very strong partisanship?

❏ 1 Strong
❏ 2 Not strong
❏ 3 (Don't know/Refused)

(ASK IF INDEPENDENT/OTHER/DON'T KNOW/REFUSED ABOVE) Do you think of yourself as closer to the (ROTATE DEMOCRATIC/REPUBLICAN) Democratic or Republican Party?

❏ 1 Closer to Democrats ❏ 3 (Neither/independent)
❏ 2 Closer to Republicans ❏ 4 (Don't know/Refused)

Thinking in political terms, would you say that you are (ROTATE CONSERVATIVE/ LIBERAL—KEEP MODERATE IN THE MIDDLE)

Conservative, Moderate, or Liberal?

❏ 1 Conservative ❏ 3 Liberal
❏ 2 Moderate ❏ 4 (Don't know/Refused)

Regardless of how you are registered, which of the following statements would you say best describes you? (ROTATE DEMOCRATIC AND REPUBLICAN STATEMENTS)

❏ 1 You almost always vote for Democratic candidates
❏ 2 You vote for Democrats more often than you vote for Republicans
❏ 3 You vote for Republicans more often than you vote for Democrats
❏ 4 You almost always vote for Republican candidates
❏ 5 (Vote equally for Democrats and Republicans)
❏ 6 (Don't know/refused)

Source: Greenberg, Quinlan, Rosner Research.

USING TARGETING INFORMATION

Once campaigns identify base supporters and persuadable voters, they need to develop a plan for reaching them. Depending on the campaign's financial resources, the typical strategy combines broadcast communication (television and radio) with direct contact (mail, e-mail, telephone calls, and door-to-door canvassing) to reach voters. Campaigns track the relative success of these communication efforts throughout the course of the campaign, making adjustments if their communications strategy fails to move persuadable voters, or if any vacillation appears among base supporters.

While this process appears relatively straightforward, it is actually quite complicated. Often there is a mismatch between the sophisticated targeting recommendations derived from partisan and historical analysis, polling data, and the actual lists of voters available to the campaigns. Voter files maintained by list vendors and state party organizations often contain limited information on individual voters (little is typically included beyond party, gender, age, geography, and sometimes race), so while a campaign's polling might indicate that it should target college-educated women, voter lists may not actually contain important demographic information such as education level. Therefore the campaign finds itself in the unfortunate situation of knowing it needs to reach college-educated women but being unable to identify them in the electorate. Some vendors do enhance their lists with census tract information, which does contain indicators of socioeconomic status, but these data are not generated at the individual level.

MICRO-TARGETING

Micro-targeting is the most recent technological innovation that allows campaigns to overcome some of the limitations of traditional targeting. In *Applebee's America*, Douglas Sosnik, Matthew Dowd, and Ron Fournier recount the moment that Bush campaign officials Matthew Dowd and Karl Rove realized that they needed to target Republican voters more effectively.[12] After Bush lost the popular vote in 2000, his strategists determined that the Republican Party needed to increase the number of reliably Republican voters in the electorate and communicate with them more effectively if they were going to compete with Democrats in future elections. (Historically, Democrats tended to employ more effective and efficient strategies of getting their core supporters to the polls; these strategies were coordinated both by the party and allied organizations such as labor unions.)

Targeting, in the view of Dowd and Rove, needed to move beyond demographics and geography to focus on lifestyle. Taking a page from commercial marketing practices; Dowd and Rove believed that they could target voters by grouping them, not by demographics or geography, but by their lifestyles. Their idea was that consumer choices (such as automobile purchases) are predictive of political behavior, such that the driver of a small hybrid car might vote Democratic while the driver of a pickup truck might vote Republican. In the authors' account, "the Bush team knew how [voters] had voted in past elections and could predict with 90 percent certainty how they would vote in 2004" by knowing their favorite vacation spots, magazines, music, sports, and the like.[13]

The ideas and technology that underlie micro-targeting in politics come directly from the world of consumer marketing. Consumer database companies such as Claritas, InfoUSA, and Axiom collect data on consumers ranging from telephone service to mortgage rates. They also gather data related to lifestyle such as car ownership, hobbies, and pet ownership. Consumer researchers mine and model the data found in these databases to segment consumers into distinct groups with particular preferences they believe are related to purchasing decisions. By drawing lists from key segments of the population, companies can market their products directly to potential customers through the mail, on the phone, or online.

In politics, consultants who work with parties and campaigns are engaged in a similar endeavor. Using consumer data along with the traditional information sources such as voter lists, voter IDs, and census and polling data, consultants are creating massive databases of the American electorate. The Republican National Committee's VoterVault, by all accounts, contains records on 165 million American voters.[14] Both political parties—as well as a range of interest groups—used these databases in 2004 and 2006 to model the electorate in the most politically competitive states.

Using these voter databases, analysts develop models to predict particular political behaviors important for voter targeting, such as being a strong partisan or a persuadable voter. This process works by drawing a sample from the databases that contain voter information, census information, and consumer information, conducting a survey gauging voters' political attitudes and preferences, and then using these results to model key political outcomes. These modeling exercises require very large sample sizes—typically a minimum of 5,000 voters, although surveys of 10,000 to 15,000 voters are not unusual. The results of this modeling are then mapped back into larger voter databases, overcoming the previous limitations of voter files that contain only partial information.

Campaigns can draw lists of base and persuadable voters from these lists and contact them directly through the mail, over the phone, and at their front doors. Equally as important, this contact can include *customized* messaging that inevitably will be much more precise than advertising over the airways. Campaigns are finding it quite effective to communicate with narrowly defined subsets of voters in ways that are tailored specifically to their unique set of concerns.

CONCLUSION

While targeting significantly increases the efficiency of voter contact by campaigns, it is far from perfect. Traditional and new targeting methods yield lists of base and persuadable voters, but these groups are never "pure." No group of base voters casts 100 percent of their ballots for the same candidate; as much as 35–40 percent inevitably will support the candidate's opponent. Similarly, persuadable groups always include significant numbers of voters who are actually *not* persuadable. Some persuadable voters may be ticket splitters, for example, but not actually open to changing their vote choice.

Voter targeting is as much an art as it is a science. It is a subjective exercise that requires campaign strategists to make educated guesses about what combination of base and persuadable groups will allow the candidate to finish first past the post. Moreover, the effectiveness of targeting is only as good as the resources campaigns put behind it. Campaigns need to have enough money to communicate with the people they categorize as their base and persuadable voters. Equally as important, campaigns must target the right message to the right voters. Base voters should not get a message designed to persuade voters. Likewise, persuadable voters should not receive the base message (unless, of course, research determines that there is some overlap between base and persuadable voters). Without resources and well-informed messaging, even the most sophisticated targeting strategy cannot guarantee a win on Election Day.

NOTES

[1]Matt Bai, "The Multilevel Marketing of the President," *New York Times Magazine* (April 25, 2004): 43–45.

[2]Of course, this strategy was not particularly effective in 2006, when the GOP continued to perform well among its base supporters but lost badly among swing groups such as Independent voters. According to exit polls, Republican candidates lost among Independent voters by 18 points.

[3]Hal Malchow, *The New Political Targeting* (Washington, DC: Campaigns and Elections, 2003).

[4]As Malchow (2003) notes, it is equally important to determine the turnout probabilities of base voters. When targeting base voters, campaigns want to focus on the voters who are least likely to vote, focusing their efforts on getting them to the polls.

[5]Bruce E. Keith, David B. Magleby, Candice J. Nelson, Elizabeth Orr, Mark C. Westlye, and Raymond E. Wolfinger, *The Myth of the Independent Voter* (Berkeley: University of California Press, 1992); Warren E. Miller and J. Merrill Shanks, *The New American Voter* (Cambridge, MA: Harvard University Press, 1996).

[6]Most of the data in this chapter come from the Voter News Service (VNS) exit polls and the Edison/Mitoftsy National Election Pool (NEP), except where otherwise noted. VNS was founded in 1993 as a consortium owned by ABC, the Associated Press, NBC, CBS, CNN, and Fox to provide conclusive, accurate, and efficient exit polling for major elections. To deal with the problems that arose with the VNS system in 2000 and 2002, ABC, AP, CBS, CNN, Fox, and NBC created the National Election Pool to provide tabulated vote counts and exit poll surveys in 2004 for major presidential primaries and the general election. These six major news organizations used Edison Media Research and Mitofsky International as the provider of exit polls. Nationally, they interviewed 13,660 respondents on Election Day in 2004 and 13,208 respondents in 2006.

[7]Anna Greenberg and Kenneth Wald, "Still Liberal After All These Years," in *Jews in American Politics*, eds. L. Sandy Maisel and Ira Forman (Lanham, MD: Rowman and Littlefield, 2001); Stanley B. Greenberg, *The Two Americas* (New York: Thomas Dunne, 2004): 120–121.

[8]Greenberg (2004): 110–114.

[9]Miller and Shanks (1996).

[10]Keith et al. (1992).

[11]Elaine Sherman, "Direct Marketing: How Does it Work for Political Campaigns?" in *Handbook of Political Marketing*, ed. Bruce I. Newman (Thousand Oaks, CA: Sage, 1999).

[12]Douglas B. Sosnik, Matthew J. Dowd, and Ron Fournier, *Applebee's America* (New York: Simon and Schuster, 2006). Using sophisticated modeling in the campaign world, however, is not a new development. Before the last decade, however, it was used primarily for donor prospecting.

[13]Sosnik, Dowd, and Fournier (2006): 34.

[14]See Sosnik, Dowd, and Fournier (2006).

INDEX

A

AARP, 116
abortion, attitudes on
  income and, 65–69
  marital status and, 33
  religious tradition and, 43
affirmative action, 77
African Americans
  attitudes on affirmative action for, 77
  future political behavior of, 20–21
  group-based heuristics among, 18–19
  political behavior of, 16–17
  religion and politics among, 41
  in urban populations, 78
  voting differences between whites and,
    10–12
age
  generation gap in, 5
  grouping people by, 109–13
  see also generation gap
American Association for Single People, 37
American Beauty (film), 81
American National Election Studies (ANES)
  abortion data of, 65
  candidates personal traits data of, 103–5
  gender gap data of, 92, 97
  generation gap data of, 116–18
  income and social class data of, 59–61
  on job satisfaction among rural employees,
    82–83
  "marriage gap" data of, 32–36, 38
  rural-urban gap data of, 74
  on "security moms," 100–101
  "worship attendance gap" data of, 44–46
Amish in the City (television series), 81
Appalachia, 89
Asian Americans, 12

B

"baby boom" generation, 111–13, 126
Barker, Lucius, 17, 20
Bartels, Larry, 19, 82, 90
base voters, 130–33
Bell, Daniel, 55
Boys Don't Cry (film), 81
Brady Bunch, The (television series), 30
Brandon, Teena, 81
Burnham, Walter Dean, 111
Bush, George H.W., 45
Bush, George W.
  ANES data on personal evaluations
    of, 103–5
  in election of 2000, 62

  evangelical Protestant and Catholic vote
    for, 43
  "gaps" in vote for in 2004, 2–6
  generational differences in support for,
    116–19
  "marriage gap" in vote for, 24
  support for among southern white women,
    102–3
  support for among women, 101
  worship attendance gap and vote for, 47

C

campaigns, targeting voters in, 129–42
Cauchon, Dennis, 25
Christian Coalition, 44
Christian Right, 43–44
cities, *see* urban populations
civil rights, 13
  legislation on, 18, 78
civil rights movement, 17
class, *see* social class
class gap, 4
Clinton, Bill, 35, 101, 118
  impeachment of, 72–73n48
congressional elections
  of 2002, 53
  of 2006, 50, 134, 143n2
  marriage gap in, 25
conservatism and conservatives
  age correlated with, 109–11
  among rural voters, 79, 89
  culture wars issues and, 63–64
  "marriage gap" and, 33
  religious traditions and, 42–43
  values issues replacing class issues
    for, 56
  worship attendance correlated with,
    41, 48
consumer marketing, 141
Converse, Philip, 15
crossover voting (ticket-splitting), 131, 135
culture war issues, 54, 55
  abortion as, 65–68
  gender gap and, 97
  social class division on, 63–64

D

Dawson, Michael, 18
Dean, Howard, 74
Deliverance (film), 81
Democracy Corps, 32, 33, 37
Democratic Leadership Council (DLC),
  53–54